# 90
## DAYS
### WITH
## JESUS

*Paul and Simmons,
Blessings on you
and yours.
Brad*

# 90 DAYS WITH JESUS

## A GUIDE FOR GROWTH

COLLECTED AND EDITED BY

### BRAD OLSEN

revolworks.com

## ILLUMIFY
**MEDIA.COM**

Copyright © 2022 by Brad Olsen

All rights reserved. No part of this book may be reproduced in any form or by any means—whether electronic, digital, mechanical, or otherwise—without permission in writing from the publisher, except by a reviewer, who may quote brief passages in a review.

Unless otherwise specified all Scripture is from New American Standard Bible®, Copyright © 1960, 1971, 1977, 1995, 2020 by The Lockman Foundation. All rights reserved. Scripture marked NIV from Holy Bible, New International Version®, NIV® Copyright ©1973, 1978, 1984, 2011 by Biblica, Inc.® Used by permission. All rights reserved worldwide. Scripture marked ESV from The Holy Bible, English Standard Version. ESV® Text Edition: 2016. Copyright © 2001 by Crossway Bibles, a publishing ministry of Good News Publishers. Scripture taken from the New King James Version®. Copyright © 1982 by Thomas Nelson. Used by permission. All rights reserved.

The views and opinions expressed in this book are those of the author and do not necessarily reflect the official policy or position of Illumify Media Global.

Published by
Revolworks Publishing
Illumify Media Global
www.IllumifyMedia.com
*"Let's bring your book to life!"*

Paperback ISBN: 978-1-955043-84-7

Typeset by Art Innovations (http://artinnovations.in/)
Cover design by Debbie Lewis

*Printed in the United States of America*

## CONTENTS

| INTRODUCTION | VII |
| --- | --- |
| LOVE | 1 |
| PRAYER | 101 |
| THE WORK OF GOD | 132 |
| THE KINGDOM OF GOD | 181 |
| THE HOLY SPIRIT | 185 |
| OTHER TOPICS | 205 |

## INTRODUCTION

How would you organize the best material to cause its readers to grow spiritually? Such was the goal of a small group of writers fifteen years ago. A group of talented interns learning to be spiritual leaders set out to create a devotional that would lend itself to applying Jesus' most important teachings from the Scriptures. I cherry-picked five of the best writers from our postgraduate internship program: Adam Boyd, Amy Laughlin Williams, Karen Simmons, Hollis Barth, and Liz Doescher. The goal was to create a book that would distill some of Jesus' most profound teachings and describe them on a single page. We started with a devotional title, followed by a clever quote, and three scripture passages. Those were followed by a page of commentary and concluded with engaging discussion questions.

We wrote extensively through several years to create this guide. We tested the devotionals on our website revolworks.com. Over time, we massaged the writings and paired them down to 180 of the best ones.

Through that effort we came up with two volumes of devotionals. This is the first volume. Whether used as a guide for a small group or a daily devotional, these thoughts should transform your understanding of Jesus and his favorite topics. Looking back through history we realize that there are relatively few great leaders, and none of them live up to the life, teachings, and leadership of Jesus of Nazareth.

Feel free to use this guide as a daily devotional or as weekly outline for your group. Either way, we hope and pray that you will be challenged and encouraged by this exercise.

# LOVE

**DAY 1**

# LOVE IS A PERSON

"We have to restore the meaning of the word 'love.' We have been using it in a careless way. When we say, 'I love hamburgers,' we are not talking about love. We are talking about our appetite, our desire for hamburgers. We should not dramatize our speech and misuse words like that. We make words like 'love' sick that way. We have to make an effort to heal our language by using words carefully."

—THICH NHAT HAHN

| 1 Corinthians 13 | 1 John 4:8-10 | John 10:17-18 |

Jesus is God, and God is Love. If we replace "love" with "Jesus" in this passage from the Apostle Paul, here is what we get:

> *If I speak with the tongues of men and of angels, but do not have [Jesus], I am a noisy gong or a clanging cymbal. If I have the gift of prophecy and know all mysteries and all knowledge; and if I have all faith, so as to remove mountains, but do not have [Jesus], I am nothing. And if*

*I give all my possessions to feed the poor, and if I surrender my body to be burned, but do not have [Jesus], it profits me nothing.*

*[Jesus] is patient, [Jesus] is kind and is not jealous; [Jesus] does not brag and is not arrogant, does not act unbecomingly; [He] does not seek [His] own, is not provoked, does not take into account a wrong suffered, [Jesus] does not rejoice in unrighteousness, but rejoices in the truth; [Jesus] bears all things, believes all things, hopes all things, endures all things.*

*[Jesus] never fails; but if there are gifts of prophecy, they will be done away; if there are tongues, they will cease; if there is knowledge, it will be done away. For we know in part and we prophesy in part, but when the perfect comes, the partial will be done away. When I was a child, I used to speak like a child, think like a child, reason like a child; when I became a man, I did away with childish things. For now we see in a mirror dimly, but then face to face; now I know in part, but then I will know fully just as I have been fully known. But now faith, hope, and [Jesus] abide these three; but the greatest of these is [Jesus].*

Brad

---

- Do you believe that love is a person?
- How do you feel reading Jesus' name in place of the word *love*?
- Which statements do you question?

## DAY 2

# GREEK TO ME

"There is no word in our language which has been so much misused and prostituted as the word love . . . It has been made so empty that for many people love may mean no more than that two people have lived together for twenty years just without fighting more often than once a week."

—ERICH FROMM

| Ephesians 4:15 | John 15:13 | 1 John 3:16 |

What does love look like?
Buying your wife flowers on a whim?
Loaning your car to a friend in need?
Calling your grandmother just to ask about her day?
Paying for the groceries of the single mother behind you in line?
All are good answers, but they fall short of defining what Jesus asks of us when He commands us to love in the new commandment.

In English the concept of the word *love* gets murky. In the English language all the linguistic conceptions of affection are rolled up into one *L* word that most of us associate with the feeling you get before you get married, the same one you'll probably lose a few years later. This is not the highest purpose to which Jesus is calling us. Something must be getting lost in translation.

The Greeks grasp the many different tones of the word *love*, depending on the meaning intended:

- *Eros* is sexual love and the root of the word *erotic*.
- *Philea* is the love among brothers or friends.
- *Storge* is the love felt for family.
- *Agape* is self-emptying love.

Which one was Jesus talking about so much in the New Testament? He was not speaking of *eros*, the fleeting feeling. He was speaking of *agape* love, the love He gives to us (and in turn asks us to give to our neighbor) is self-sacrificial. It is when a person lays down his or her life for another person: if not once on a cross, then in small doses daily.

What does *agape* look like?

It looks uncomfortable.

It looks risky.

It looks like skin in the game.

Whatever the manifestation, though never a one-size-fits-all concept, it always requires a step outside the comfort zone. What the comfort zone looks like depends on the one attempting to love:

For a peacemaker, love looks like honesty.

For a challenger, love looks like following someone else's lead.

For a perfectionist, love looks like letting go of control.

*Hollis*

———•———

- **What does uncomfortable love look like for you?**
- **Who has been an example of agape love in your life?**
- **Who is someone in your daily life who could use some of this love?**

# DAY 3

# ACTIVATION

"We have done so much,
with so little, for so long, that now we can
do anything with nothing."

—ANONYMOUS

| Matthew 25:31-40 | John 15:9-15 | John 13:1 |

Have you ever made a major life change and then found yourself in a less-than-ideal situation? Your new boss has a screw loose. Your new neighbors don't have nearly the same funny friend-group potential as your last ones. Your new lunch buddies are stiff and boring compared to your last workplace. The task or location itself was an upgrade, but the people that came with it are a bummer.

When we reach decision points in life, we make cost-benefit assessments. Whatever the material benefit, though, it is hard to overestimate the effects of the people involved in your environment. Relationships may be intangible, yet they are vitally important to our well-being.

When our new relationships grow slower compared to the easy, natural connection of old ones, it can be disheartening. Sometimes the issue lies not with the loser in the cubicle next to us, but with the person in ours. The way Jesus built a team out of a rag-tag assortment of average joes encourages us to bloom where planted, no matter how unnatural the soil might seem.

The disciples weren't great guys to begin with. Jesus activated them. He spent time with them, talked to them about their dreams, listened to their fears. He loved them, transforming them into a force to be reckoned with.

He says that we have this power, and obligation, too: "Love one another, just as I have loved you" (John 13:34 NLT). With His example, we are equipped to activate those in our environment, dissolving superficial social barriers in the process. We bring the love, after seeing how He loved. He does the rest. How it blesses the Father to see His children loving one another.

*Hollis*

---

- **What is your biggest fear about new friendships?**
- **What mental fences are you using to rule out potential friendships?**
- **Who could you befriend?**

# DAY 4

# SMILE BACK

"You can have the other words: chance, luck, coincidence, serendipity. I'll take grace. I don't know what it is exactly, but I'll take it."

—MARY OLIVER

| Zephaniah 3:17-20 | Isaiah 49:14-16 | 1 John 3:1-3 |

Jenny hunches over the crib, using her hands to spread her eyes wide so they're comically large. "I'm gonna give myself wrinkles before my time," she whispers as she contorts her eyebrows up and stretches her cheeks into a fish face, wiggling her fingers with her thumbs in her ears.

Her little one, lying on a blanket beneath her, just blinks. Weeks and weeks of making crazy faces and embarrassing baby sounds, there is still no response. "Anybody in there?" she coos after her fourth attempt at peekaboo of the morning.

The baby looks up. Noticing something odd about her wild gestures, he cocks his head to the side curiously. And slowly, slowly, a toothless smile spreads across his face. He gurgles.

Finally, some recognition! This small expression of joy on her child's face is nothing, though, compared to the deep and lasting joy Jenny is experiencing in this moment—a confirmation of the unbreakable bond between parents and their one-of-a-kind creation.

God sees His children the same way. He expresses His love for us in the smiles of strangers when we're feeling isolated, a breathtaking sunset on a long commute home, a still morning in the midst of a family crisis. He orchestrates conversations with others at just the right time. When we couldn't picture how it was all going to work out, it simply does, unfolding better than we could have planned.

What a relief that someone bigger than us—someone who knows the hairs on our head and when we rise up and lie down—is working on our behalf. One of the strongest forces in mankind, a mother's love for her child, pales in comparison to the way the Creator feels about His creation. And He's telling us, every day. Sometimes through a sunset, sometimes through a contract. But always for our good.

*Hollis*

---

- Can you see the way God smiles at you, or are you missing it?
- Do you feel loved enough by God to smile back?
- What might God be doing in your life to get your attention?

**DAY 5**

# THE LOSERS

"A man who loves others based solely on how they make him feel, or what they do for him, is really not loving others at all—but loving only himself."

—CRISS JAMI

| Luke 5:1-11 | Luke 22 | Romans 12:14 |

Looking at their track records, Jesus really didn't do such a great job of picking his followers . . . or did He?

Peter (the Rock) disowned Him. Thomas doubted Him. The brothers James and John bickered about who would be the greatest and who deserved the honor of sitting at Jesus' right hand in the coming kingdom. And Judas betrayed Him.

Do you think Jesus was a bad judge of character and picked duds by mistake? The Scriptures say that Jesus "Himself knew what was in a man" (John 2:25). In the Hebrew understanding of the word *knew*, it means He could see inside everyone and know the blackness of each one's heart.

With this in mind, is there any evidence of Jesus treating any of the disciples differently because of their particular evil predisposition? Nope. He loved each one of them, right down to washing their feet (just before Judas went out to betray him).

Throughout Jesus' life, and despite the wickedness with which men (even His friends) treated Him, he never grew cynical. He kept on loving them despite intimate knowledge of their shortcomings that would ultimately prove fatal to Him. Ouch! The Scriptures say He "was not entrusting Himself to them" (John 2:24), yet He continued to give His followers unconditional love.

And He left that as our example: "Love one another; just as I have loved you" (John 13:34).

There we have it. Protect your heart from being calloused. Continue to love, even when someone you care about hurts you deeply. Find someone whom no one else seems to love, especially if they're unpopular, unsuccessful, unattractive, or strange. Remember that people *will* hurt you. But allow Jesus' grace to shield you from letting it harden you. Ask for it when you feel walls of self-protection rising up. Be on guard for them.

Then, when we're all together again in heaven, He'll say to us:

> *"Come, you who are blessed by my Father, inherit the kingdom prepared for you from the foundation of the world. For I was hungry, and you gave Me something to eat; I was thirsty, and you gave Me something to drink; I was a stranger, and you invited Me in; naked and you clothed Me; I was sick, and you visited Me; I was in prison, and you came to Me" (Matthew 25: 34-36).*

Amen.

*Brad*

- Who in your orbit have you shut out because of hurt?
- What qualities in others do you find hardest to love?
- What defense mechanisms do you use to protect yourself from those who have hurt you?

# DAY 6

# PERSON OF LOVE

"Hope begins in the dark, the stubborn hope that if you just show up and try to do the right thing, the dawn will come. You wait and watch and work: you don't give up."

—ANNE LAMOTT

| 1 Corinthians 13 | John 8:1-11 | John 15:12-17 |

Who really expects love to deliver anymore? We hear the word everywhere, but we also see the reality in the same places.

Another woman meets a guy she likes. He's separated from his wife, and the two begin dating. She moves in with him, as he plans to divorce his wife. Three years later, she's waiting on him to divorce his wife and marry her.

Pearl Jam's song "Better Man" encapsulates this acceptance of non-love.

On one hand she scoffs, and thinks, "Yeah, right, like there's nothing better." Yet her fears remain, telling her, "There really is nothing better for you."

Look at the Apostle Paul's description of love in 1 Corinthians 13. How many people do you know who love like that?

Look at Jesus' understanding of it. He washes His students' feet. He forgives their failures but refuses to allow them to remain fledgling. One of those students identifies himself as "the disciple whom Jesus loved" (John 13:23 NIV). He and ten others watched love, listened to love, and experienced love changing them. They then proceeded to live and die for love, for Jesus.

We think of such love like Paul mentions and Jesus demonstrates the way we do magic: charming, but we see the dull and numbing realities facing us. Those include routine, few surprises, and a begrudging acceptance of what we settle for.

What then? Do we continue with hearts half asphyxiated by boredom and life's depression? Or could we too begin to listen and watch for love to change us? Might it really exist? Could Jesus actually know something we don't?

Let's take a chance. Let's examine the Nazarene. What do we have to lose? This lack of faith, hope, love? We know that's not life, and we are dying wanting it.

*Adam*

---

- **What do you believe love is?**
- **Have you experienced what you believe?**
- **How do your beliefs about love compare with those of Paul and Jesus?**

# DAY 7

# GIVING FROM NOTHING

"I must reduce myself until I am a mere conscious man, I must fundamentally renounce possessions of all kinds, not to save my soul, but in order to follow Jesus."

—OSWALD CHAMBERS

| Mark 12:35-44 | Mark 10:13-31 | Matthew 5:38-48 |

Viktor Frankl describes the experience of nakedness in Auschwitz, a World War II Nazi concentration camp. When he had nothing—truly nothing—death no longer held fear over him. By this time, he had lost his family, his career, his strength, his money, his possessions, his house, his clothing, and his identity. The Nazis reduced him to a walking skeleton who answered to a number. Only then could he face death without wincing, knowing he had nothing to lose.

Reading Frankl's book, *Man's Search for Meaning*, prompts the question: "Do you think it's easier to love when you have nothing?" The question may seem unique to a twenty-first century American.

But it's not original. Since the first century, followers of Jesus embraced poverty, believing that He demanded it. The earliest witnesses reported, "And all those who had believed were together and had all things in common; and they began selling their property and possessions, and were sharing them with all, as anyone might have need" (Acts 2:44-45). Early believers chose freedom from a life directed by and devoted to the acquisition of wealth. This tradition reaches through the ages to St. Francis of Assisi, St. Ignatius of Loyola, and, most recently, to Mother Teresa. Yet we find it seldom today.

Jesus watched as a poor widow placed her two small copper coins into the temple treasury. Added together, they totaled less than a penny. Few of us would bother to pick them up on the sidewalk. Yet Jesus identifies her gift as the most precious. She gave out of her poverty.

We need to be free to give, and we tend to give better when we have less. Giving a small amount is easier than giving a large one. Jesus asks us to give freely and understand that God Himself will care for each of us.

So it is with love. The most precious gift is the time spent with someone when we are at our busiest, the $20 given to the beggar when we didn't have it to spare, the effort lent to a neighbor when we are most tired, or a moment of pause to ponder our maker in the midst of chaos.

*Brad*

- Do you give from your excess or out of your charity?
- Do I love from my excess or out of my charity?
- How did Jesus love and give?

# DAY 8

# GOD IS LOVE

*"In His holy flirtation with the world,
God occasionally drops a handkerchief.
These handkerchiefs are called saints."*

—FREDERICK BUECHNER

| 1 Corinthians 13 | 1 John 4:7-21 | Jeremiah 31:3 |

When a friend heard 1 Corinthians 13 for the first time, she asked, "That's in the Bible?"

"Absolutely," I replied. "It's rather well known."

"Wow!" she said, "I never would have thought the Bible was so familiar."

Upon hearing this, my first reaction was, "Where've you been all your life?" But after further reflection, this exchange highlighted a flaw in our common understanding.

We imagine love as personal and personalized; we don't think of love being a person. The apostle John asserts that "God is love" (1 John 4:8) and that sounds pleasant. We then distinguish between God being love and love not being a god, the result of which has some theological and philosophical import. Still, we want orthodoxy.

Worship God alone and know that He is love or loving. That makes more sense, right? Because we want to focus on God and not just on love. But there's the rub.

My friend missed this important aspect of love, and so do we. We look at love and see an idea, a feeling, and in our loftiest moments, a commitment. Poems, songs, novels, and movies have solidified such thinking. Yet John the apostle says love is an actual person. This idea runs counter to our thinking; and even if it didn't, we certainly wouldn't think of the God of the Old Testament as being love. The Old Testament focuses on war and wrath, and not on God's unrequited love.

Yet the Scriptures plead this case: God Himself is love, and when we read with fresh eyes, we see that Jesus personifies love more than anything we've yet seen. Try substituting the name "Jesus" each time you read "love" in 1 Corinthians 13. The alignment stuns and then resonates. "Jesus is patient. Jesus is kind, Jesus is not jealous; Jesus does not brag; he is not arrogant."

People from all backgrounds and faiths hold something akin to affection for Jesus. Perhaps when they find Jesus, His life, and His words coincide with their experiences of love? Perhaps what we secretly desire when we speak of love is the person of Jesus?

We've mentioned that the purpose of life is love. C. S. Lewis said he was startled to discover that the universe's center existed not in some place, but in a person. If so, then purpose comes together in a person, who is love. We find purpose in love, and we find love in Jesus. His invitation to follow Him now grows exceedingly attractive: "Come and see" is a summons to step into our life's purpose, into love, into a life with Jesus.

*Adam*

- What comes to mind as you consider love?
- What do you see when you look at Jesus? How do His words affect you?
- How would following Jesus' teachings impact your life?

**DAY 9**

# HE JUST LOVED ME THERE

*"Isn't it interesting that the one person who never suffered from a Messiah complex was the Messiah himself?"*

—PHILIP YANCEY

| John 13:5-20 | 2 Corinthians 3 |

Have you seen the protestors who attend the funerals of fallen soldiers? Their banners scream, "GOD HATES YOU!" "YOU'RE GOING TO HELL!"? They protest against government policies. They claim God punishes by death in battle. They claim they stand against immorality and godlessness. Few have responded favorably to them or their tactics.

Something similar used to occur in Memphis on Saturday nights. A group of people would march through infamous Beale Street carrying banners. These banners told of impending doom due to the debauchery lifestyle of the bars and clubs. The group handed out fear-inducing tracts while sermonizing through megaphones. While not as malicious as the funeral protestors, these people provoked a kindred response: alienation, disgust, confusion.

Obviously, these people want to convey what they perceive as God's displeasure with certain lifestyle choices. Yes, they may only convey their own displeasure, but they think they do what's right. They also, when their motives remain pure, seek to encourage others to change.

When we want others to change, we scold, yell, condemn, push, and cajole them into what we believe is best. This although we sometimes miss what is best for anyone. But was this Jesus' way?

To the woman caught in adultery, Jesus said, "I do not condemn you, either. Go. From now on do not sin any longer" (John 8:11). To Thomas, the disciple who couldn't believe Jesus had returned, Jesus said, "Place your finger here, and see My hands; and take your hand and put it into My side; and do not continue in disbelief, but be a believer" (John 20:27). To the chief tax collector Zacchaeus, Jesus said, "today I must stay at your house" (Luke 19:5). To a woman who lived a wanton life, Jesus told her, "I have food to eat that you do not know about" (John 4:32). To James and John, who wanted to call down fire on people, He said that He "did not come to destroy men's lives but to save them" (Luke 9:56 NKJV).

This way stands in contrast to our own.

Jesus' acceptance of people didn't offer them a license to sin or to continue in it. Rather, His love moved them to desire change. He didn't leave them where they were; He loved them where they were, and in doing so He loved them to freedom. This kind of love challenges us because we esteem cutthroat fairness and stringent justice. We fear that such love will lead only to tolerance, not to change.

Jesus understood that people require the messy work of love. To chastise, however, is easier and cheaper. But love takes much time, enduring patience, courageous acceptance, and a bold willingness. Perhaps love will eventually alter the way a person behaves and lives. But perhaps not. We are called to love without a finish line.

At the end of any day, all we can control is how we respond to others, how we engage the world. How we do so matters much more than how others behave. I cannot control how you behave. But with Jesus loving me here, where I am, I might be able to love you where you are. And that makes all the difference.

*Adam*

---

- **Think of one friend who habitually does something of which you disapprove. How have you talked to this person about his or her behavior?**
- **What response have you seen?**
- **Does your approach look like Jesus'?**

## DAY 10

# THE WHOLE WORLD WILL KNOW

*"Alexander, Charlemagne, and I have founded empires. But on what did we rest the creation of our genius? Upon force. Jesus Christ founded his empire upon love; and at this hour millions of men would die for him."*

—NAPOLEON BONAPARTE

| Zephaniah 3:17-20 | Isaiah 49:14-16 | 1 John 3:1-3 |

Jesus said God wanted to save the world. He then taught His followers to love one another. That was His master plan: love.

Jesus said the world will know that God sent Him if His followers have "complete unity" (John 17:23 NIV).

All this borders on unbelievable, so we skip over it. Whether we hope to save souls or feed the hungry, we trust our methods. Napoleon had his force, and we have ours: training seminars, convincing arguments, marketing campaigns, stylish bracelets, catchy slogans, pet dogmas. Sometimes we pull out the big weapons: petitions and demonstrations. Some people seem to believe action and activism will change hearts, and usher in utopia.

The most revolutionary leaders in the world taught the most subversive and simple of all acts: love. Jesus, Gandhi, and Martin Luther King Jr. chose love as their central premise as well. In the face of violence: love. In the face of persecution: love. In the face of discrimination, oppression, and subjugation: love. Fight fire with water. Their droplet of love in time's pond sent ripples into lives everywhere.

The great revolutionary dreamers—Marx, Che Guevara, Hitler, Woodrow Wilson—have all come up short. Activists everywhere—on college campuses and on Capitol Hill—all possess conviction and passion, yet they lack the one great weapon of mass instruction: love.

The movie *Pay It Forward* brilliantly painted this picture. A social studies teacher gives an assignment to his junior high class to think of an idea to change the world. One student creates a plan for paying forward favors. In turn, the lad not only affects the life of his single mother but sets in motion a wave of human kindness.

You see, if we begin loving people and teaching them to do the same, a movement of magnitude can lend light to the world's dark night. It can touch people everywhere, starting with you.

We need not do away with our methods of touching lives, feeding the hungry, ending war, fighting disease and poverty. But we cannot hope for any real success in these arenas without love. If we want to save the world, could we imagine any act more powerful than loving neighbors in need, or enemies who revile us? If we want to reach the world, can we fathom any more convincing evidence of deity than laying down our lives for others?

*Adam*

---

- **How would you change the world?**
- **What, exactly, is love?**
- **Why is it so revolutionary?**

# DAY 11

# THE COMMANDMENT

"If the shoe doesn't fit, must we change the foot?"

—GLORIA STEINEM

| 1 John 3 | 1 John 4 | John 15 |

I fail at love. As soon as it costs me something, I check out. And this is frustrating, because Jesus demands love. That's really it.

Two friends come to mind. Both exhaust me, taxing my mental and emotional resources. Something in each—whether upbringings, characters, attitudes, or habits—keeps me from easy, casual, Sunday-afternoon-of-golf appreciation of them.

The first guy redefines long-winded. He talks more, and more loudly, than anyone I've met. He possesses no inside voice. Not in restaurants, business meetings, people's homes, government offices, or in dealing with the opposite sex. He's never on time. He is, however, overwhelmingly kind, generous, patient, knowledgeable, and humble.

The second guy curses like a sailor, treats friends roughly, boasts and alienates. He's known for selfishness and pleasure-seeking. The list goes on, but in truth, he cares deeply for his friends. The rest is a façade, and sometimes due to his immaturity. That is what breaks my affection and tolerance.

The problem with both guys is . . . me. I don't have enough love. Jesus tells me to love as He has, and I can't. If I could, I'd enjoy much more fulfilling relationships with both guys. Instead, I treat each one with a degree of condescension, contempt, and inconsideration.

Work to listen to their hearts? No. Judge, criticize, and fail to understand where they are, where they've come from, and what they're dealing with? Yes.

Without Jesus' help, I'm hopeless.

These relationships, like all my others, are doomed. I cannot love like this. At some point, something in someone else pushes me away. I have no desire to move back. I need someone to push me toward the other person. Jesus keeps telling me to go back, to embrace the other person. He keeps showing me how when I connect with Him.

When men from a tribal world meet Jesus, the first thing they do is invite their wife to live in the house with them. Before, the wife lived in the stall with the animals. Jesus touches them, and they see their wives differently. They love differently.

We're supposed to be lights. Light will emanate from us, but we need a source of power. Jesus is that power. When we are connected to Him, the light radiates.

We can't help but love as it runs through us.

*Adam*

- Do you grow frustrated in your inability to love?

- Do people frustrate you because you're "just too different" from them or because you're too limited?

- Who in your life has loved you without failing you or disappointing you?

# DAY 12

# MANIFESTATIONS THROUGH MOTION

"Yes... You do.
What you tell me about in the nights.
That is not love. That is only passion and lust.
When you love you wish to do things for.
You wish to sacrifice for. You wish to serve."

—CATHERINE
TO HER POTENTIAL LOVER, HENRY,
IN ERNEST HEMINGWAY'S A FAREWELL TO ARMS

1 Corinthians 13     James 1:26-27

I was seven years old. As my mom bustled around the kitchen cleaning, I realized it. What a terrible discovery.

My confused childhood mind comprehended for the first time the conscious reality that I would have to blink and swallow for the rest of my life. My existence had only just begun, I thought to myself as I made the conscious effort, *blink and swallow, blink and swallow*. I would never realize any other dreams or aspirations for the rest of my days. My every moment and continual thoughts would have to focus on these bodily tasks, these all-too-necessary tasks.

I pondered this for several seemingly endless minutes, feeling dejected, discouraged, and depressed until my sisters hauled out the Barbie dolls.

Years later, I sit here, many dreams reached, still blinking and swallowing thanks to the genius of involuntary bodily actions. These actions occur through me and because of me but not by wearisome effort, as I once believed.

What is love?

We prefer to see it as a stagnant label placed on any feel-good emotion or a romanticized ideal. We attach it flippantly to anything we find desirable. It is expendable and temporary. A throwaway commodity. It requires no effort and no action.

Jesus' love exists in action. It exists in motion. The things we hold up as love represent the real thing no more than a plaster mold of a face represents the real face. It cannot move, it cannot grow, it cannot express emotion, or passion, or pain.

Philosopher Simone Weil said, "The first trait of love is attentiveness." To be attentive is to notice others, to care, and to react to discovered needs. When we love, we reject the idea of a stagnant, flowery ideal. We desire to sacrifice. We desire to serve.

I remember another childhood day when I did something characteristically conniving. I remember apologizing to my mom and pulling out all the stops to show my remorse. I even made a colorful construction paper card. In bold strokes of Crayola marker, I wrote, "I love you." Beaming, I presented this offering to my mom, who accepted it but then challenged me to something more. "Don't tell me, show me."

Our bodies live and carry the will to stay alive. Our hearts pump, our glands salivate and secrete, our eyes blink. This intangible force forces tangible efforts. Living causes reactions. Love produces action.

*Amy*

---

- **How do you love others?**
- **How do you feel loved?**
- **Why should you love at all?**

# DAY 13

# THE GOLDEN RULE?!

*"Nothing would be radical about
'Thou shalt love thy neighbor as thyself'
if it did not contain 'as thyself'."*

—IMMANUEL KANT

Leviticus 19:9-18   Luke 10:25-37

Shocking. Nothing less than this adequately describes Moses' teaching that Jesus echoed: "Love your neighbor as yourself."

Are you kidding?

Maybe it's just me, but one should think about it this way: each morning when you wake up, you don't debate whether to feed and clothe yourself. You just do it. You spend little time contemplating whether you should care for yourself. We all make ample time to consider our best interest. We eat healthy, or at least plentifully. We rest often. We exercise. We work to provide for ourselves and for our futures. We work hard in relationships to promote our brand.

We have missteps, such as our periodic splurging. Or we feed our addictions with another drink, smoke, or snack. But for the most part, we prioritize our own interests.

I care for me. I love me. You love you. These are givens.

Do this for another person? This seldom crosses my mind. Yes, the words "love your neighbor as yourself" have crossed my mind. But to live like that? Not so much. Maybe if it had Moses and Jesus could have saved their breath.

I say, "I love you" to a handful of people. But none occupies my mind as much as I do.

Benefit, promote, provide for, and protect another the way I do myself? That's ridiculous. Did either Jesus or Moses consider what my cost might be if I do this for another? This practice would steal my time, my money, my energy, and my efforts. And above all, who will meet my needs?

Jesus pronounces that, "Greater love has no one than this, that one lay down his life for his friends" (John 15:13). If I love my friends as I love myself, I must lay my life down for them. I'll spend my time serving them and giving to them. I'll forget about me as I focus on them; there will be little time to think about me. This is a sort of death.

But Jesus also said that whoever loses his life will save it. This makes little rational sense. Maybe when we begin to focus our love powers outward, toward others, we've then started to live. In the moment, all our love powers and capacities point to us.

That's still crazy. But it's so crazy, it just might work.

*Adam*

- **Who do you love? How so?**
- **What is the personal cost of loving another?**

# DAY 14

# THIRSTY

"Wild, wild horses couldn't drag me away"

—THE ROLLING STONES,
"WILD HORSES"

| John 4:4-42 | Luke 7:36-50 | 1 John 3:11-24 |

We thirst for love. Some say we're deficient without it. The Apostle John says God is love (1 John 4:16). If we're children of God—or at least cast in His image—and if John is right about God, love should play a key role in our lives.

The signs point this way. What percentage of popular songs depicts love? Why do women sipping margaritas at bars speak wistfully of marriage? Why do children cling to the legs of parents? Why do so many young singles give so much time and money to nightclubs? Is it just about hormones and the pursuit of sex? Why do romance novels sell so well? Does the boy from a broken home sleep with girls for the feeling or to chase something even more elusive, such as intimacy?

Studies show that babies' brain development hinges largely on the amount of touch received during their first few years. The more touch a child receives, the faster and stronger the brain capacity grows.

In the 1930s, two separate cases involving six-year-old girls who were discovered by authorities. The girls had received minimal human contact their entire lives. They had no language or social skills. The world starved these girls of love, and the deprivation crippled them.

We need love. We need touch and conversation, comfort and compassion, attention and investment. To live a fully human life, love stands next to food, water, and shelter as indispensable.

Many celebrate love and tell us of its wonders. Few, if any, can teach us anything about it. Jesus does. He teaches us how to give it, how to receive it, how to live it. He teaches us how to come fully alive, reconnecting with others and the God who is love.

He beckons us to draw near, as He did the woman at the well, and promises us living water that satisfies permanently. Jesus makes bold claims. Given our dearth of love, it's a safe bet that His metaphor of water has something to do with love.

Drinking the living water sounds better all the time.

*Adam*

---

▫ **How great in is your need for love?**

▫ **Where do you seek love?**

▫ **How do you respond to Jesus' words and examples of love?**

**DAY 15**

# FALLING? OR CHOOSING?

> "They have invented a phrase . . . `free-love'—as if a lover ever had been, or ever could be, free. It is the nature of love to bind itself, and the institution of marriage merely paid the average man the compliment of taking him at his word."
>
> —G.K. CHESTERTON

| Deuteronomy 7:7-13 | Deuteronomy 10:12-22 |

Why wedding vows? Have you ever considered this? Why does a priest, pastor, or judge ask a man, "Will you have this woman to be your wife; to live together in the covenant of marriage? Will you love her, comfort her, honor and keep her, in sickness and in health; and, forsaking all others, be faithful to her as long as you both shall live?"

Why does he ask the man to promise? Is he not in love? Won't this suffice?

Someone recently told me he'd fallen out of love with a girl. "Huh, that can happen?" I asked.

"Sure. It just wasn't there anymore."

"And you want to get married one day?"

"Definitely."

What then? If like most people, he wants to marry, how does he navigate the perils of falling in and out of love?

Like Chesterton says, love binds itself. The lover promises to be there, to do that which we call loving. Whenever we read of love in the Scriptures, we come across commands and commitments. Very little hinges on feeling. "Love so-and-so… Do this for this person… Do that for that one." Love seems to rest in the fulfilling of these acts. One performs and the other is loved.

Similarly, God, having chosen His people, speaks of His commitment to them. He makes a covenant in Genesis. The thread of this promise runs through the rest of Scripture, all the way to Revelation. He's bound himself to these people and continues to show them love, comforting, honoring, and keeping them. He remains faithful.

Commitment first.

Want proof? *Glamour* magazine recently ran an online article about making someone fall in love with you. One piece of advice: don't do something for that person. Let them do something for you. Doing something for someone increases feelings for them. The choice to act and the act itself precedes the feelings in at least one way. *Glamour* said it. Case closed.

We choose to love. We're too flooded with cultural visions of cupid striking us. Some of that predestined thinking about love seduces us, but it doesn't bind us. The free will kind of love, where we choose to make and fulfill a promise, really binds us. And sometimes makes us feel woozy.

Responsibility for love belongs to us not to the stars. Feelings ebb and flow, but neither feelings nor a fat kid with wings determine the depth of fidelity; that's merely a euphemism for cowardice.

*Adam*

---

- How do you define love?
- Why make a vow to love someone?
- **What do you think of Chesterton's assessment of love's binding itself?**

# DAY 16

# CONTRACTS AND CUTTING

"All it cost me was my whole life,
and all it gives me is everything."

—PAT GREEN, "EDEN'S GATE"

Genesis 17:9-14 | Jeremiah 9:23-26 | Mark 10:1-12

We're confused. Today, we plan for divorce before we marry. Built-in protections, such as pre-nuptial agreements, safeguard one's property in the likely event of a divorce. This kind of thinking is selfish.

How far have we strayed? Do we understand so little of love?

On Christmas Day, 1914, German and British soldiers called a cease-fire from World War I. The Germans began singing carols, and the British soon chimed in from across no-man's land. After a few carols were sung in English and German, soldiers began leaving the safety of their trenches to shake hands, exchange cigarettes as gifts, and play soccer. For a few hours, enemies risked defenselessness. After the festivities, soldiers returned to the trenches, and the war continued.

Hebrew Scriptures tell us God stamped His people as His own via circumcision. Strange, huh? The prophet Jeremiah made some sense of this. He said God wanted people to circumcise their hearts. The physical circumcision exemplified what God desired inside His people. Their most intimate part had to be cut open, bleed, and shed of its protective covering. This left it both defenseless and more sensitive.

What's the takeaway from bleeding hearts and removing protective coverings? We cannot love with armor on. The steel between us prevents any embrace. It encumbers and guards, but it never allows us to really touch each other's flesh, each other's person.

Prenups, by definition, mean defense. They hedge against a potential wound. Back in the day, a man wanting to marry a woman cut open an animal, stood in its blood, and marked his forehead with the crimson liquid. He said, "May such happen to me if I ever fail you by breaking our covenant."

He made no mention of what she owed him, nor of any effort to protect himself.

Today, prenups trump covenants. If you fail me, I keep mine. There's no mention of what I owe you. In poker-speak, I refuse to go all in. We sign our marriage contracts in pencil, our prenups in ink, and neither with blood. "May such be mine if you fail me." How backward.

Let's go back to loving without shields and armor and protective contracts. Let's risk the money, the heart, and the life. Love, real love, demands that we leave our trenches, risking everything. Rather than walk away with possessions intact, covenants demand we lose everything, even our lives, if we fail.

We can't have sex fully clothed. Who'd want to?

*Adam*

---

- What do you hold back when you love?
- What were your romantic notions as a child? Were they bold or protective and fearful?
- Do you expect someone who loves you to hold something back?

DAY 17

# THE SECOND IS LIKE IT

*"All loves should simply be steppingstones to the love of God."*

—PLATO

| James 3:9-12 | Leviticus 19:18 |

Parents will tell you. Just ask them.

How does it feel when your children get along with one another? How does it feel when they scream and fight?

There's no tension for parents like that of their children fighting. And there's no peace like a home where the kids get along. And, oh my, if children go out of their way to help one another or sacrifice something precious for someone else, parents find heaven on earth.

It's the same with God. When His children get along, care for one another, and make sacrifices, it pleases Him deeply. When they fight, it pierces His heart. When Jesus identifies the most important commandment in Matthew 22, He draws a firm line to the second: "The second is like it, 'You shall love your neighbor as yourself.' (Matt. 22:39).

The Scriptures tell us that man (and woman) was fashioned in God's image. There is something inherently God in each of us. Therefore, we are His children. Our neighbors are His children, and He wants love exhibited in each relationship.

Unkindness troubles Him.

"With [our tongue] we bless our Lord and Father; and with it we curse people, who have been made in the likeness of God." (James 3:9) When we belittle people, or curse them, we insult God Himself. Love flows from the Father, and the overflow of that love should reach those around us.

When he was eight years old, our son Jeremy made a decision. He decided that his younger brother, Ben, wanted to go to a Nebraska football game more than he did. Don't get me wrong: Jeremy yearned to attend the game, as did any normal kid in the Cornhusker state. Yet he decided to give his single ticket to Ben. When Jeremy told me what he wanted to do, everything inside me wanted to talk some sense into him.

Then I realized the power of the gift.

I told him, "It's your decision." He trotted downstairs and told his brother. I could hear the shriek when Ben learned he was going to the game. He streaked upstairs to tell me the news. His eyes beamed with excitement, as did mine: but for different reasons. My son sacrificed a precious gift of his own for his brother.

He had loved his brother, and in doing so, he had loved me.

*Brad*

---

- How do you feel when you see people insult others? Compliment them?
- If people are made in God's image, how does this change your view of people?
- How does loving people depend on your love for God?

# DAY 18

# FAITH IN LOVE

"Hope begins in the dark, the stubborn hope that if you just show up and try to do the right thing, the dawn will come. You wait and watch and work: you don't give up."

—ANNE LAMOTT

| 1 Corinthians 13 | John 8:1-11 | John 15:12-17 |

Who expects love to deliver anymore? We hear the word everywhere, but we also see the reality in the same places.

A girl was asked if she'd go on a date with someone besides the guy she was seeing. She replied, "He's not my boyfriend, but I don't want to jeopardize anything."

"Does he treat you well?"

She half-shrugged, with a resigned tilt of the head to her shoulder.

"Does he make you feel good about who you are?"

Same response.

But still she didn't want to jeopardize what she had.

The movie *Walk the Line* depicted Johnny Cash's love for June Carter. Before he married his first wife, she waited for years for him to bring his love home.

Look at the Apostle Paul's description of love in 1 Corinthians 13. How many people do you know who love like that?

Look at the Nazarene Jesus' understanding of it. He washed His students' feet. He forgave their failures but refused to allow them to remain fledgling. One of those students identified himself as "the one Jesus loves." He and ten others watched love, listened to love, and experienced love changing them. They then proceeded to live and die for love, for Jesus.

We think of love like Paul mentions, and Jesus demonstrates the way we do magic: charming, but we see the dull and numbing realities facing us. Those include routine, few surprises, and a begrudging acceptance of what we settle for.

What then? Do we continue with hearts half-asphyxiated by boredom and depression? Or could we too begin to listen and watch for love to change us? Might it really exist? Could Jesus know something we don't?

Let's take a chance. Let's look at the Nazarene. What do we have to lose? We know that life is more than just material things, and we are dying for richer lives.

*Adam*

---

- What do you believe love is?
- How have you experienced the love you believe in?
- How do your beliefs about love compare with those of Paul and Jesus?

# DAY 19

# WHICH LOVE?

"Father's Day: The man gazes at the bluish screen from the slump of his Lazy-Boy. His wife presses a young daughter to tell him that she loves him. She resists, knowing his surly nature and aversion to affection. She approaches, confronting her fear."

—GRAHAM GREENE, THE END OF THE AFFAIR

| Hosea 2 | 1 Corinthians 12:31-13:13 | 2 Corinthians 5:16-21 |

He attacks: "What the hell do you want? Don't bother me!" The father hits the girl's mother with his fists, and with words about other women; the mother responds with her own fists and stories of nights with men.

The girl watches.

This girl meets a boy. He says something about love and explains that it means sex. She says, "Okay." At fourteen. She cries on her fifteenth birthday. She's lost something. At her party, her mother forces the father to dance with his daughter.

The girl moves in with the boy. Her house is no home, and his parents treat her well. The boy begins to love other girls. Just as her father did. The girl loves other boys, like her mother.

Soon the boy and girl move to a new city, to an apartment of their own. They play grown-up. They play mature. They play love.

They break up. They come back together. They mention words of love and show it with other lovers.

Other boys want to date her. She loves them, then others.

The girl, now a young woman, meets some nice people. They talk of love. Then they tell her good things about herself. They tell her true things, some of which hurt. Yet something in her heart tells her they are true. These new friends make love look and sound different. It feels different.

The girl becomes a woman, and not just in face and form. Her habits change, both those of her heart and her tongue.

She begins to speak a new language. Her childhood vocabulary survives inside her; she spoke it for twenty years. But she's learning new words, new sentences, new responses, and new meanings. They flow from her as her new friends embrace, encourage, and forgive. Again and again.

The new language slowly replaces the old. She learns, day by day, how to approach her new Father, one who smiles as she comes near.

*Adam*

- What have you learned to associate with love from your family, society, or culture?
- Does this line up with what Paul describes as love in 1 Corinthians 13?
- How do you understand the word *love*? Why?

# DAY 20

# FACETS OF AN ELEPHANT

"And that wasn't the end of it. There are always those who take it upon themselves to defend God, as if Ultimate Reality, as if the sustaining frame of existence, were something weak and helpless."

—YANN MARTEL, LIFE OF PI

| 1 Corinthians 13 | John 11 | Romans 8:31-39 |

Gandhi relays the story of a group of blind men gathered around the elephant. Each touches a different part: one the tail, one the trunk, one the massive body, and another the tusk. Someone asked them, "What is an elephant?"

The man touching the tail described it as something thin and circular with hair on the end.

Quickly the man holding the trunk interrupted. While he agreed with the circular description, he argued that it presented itself as something thick and muscular, capable of twisting, bending, and grasping.

Half amused at his friends' misdirection and half frustrated by their ignorance, the man with his hand on the body attempted to enlighten his companions. He described the elephant as something huge and leathery. It stood solidly immovable and towering so much so that he could not reach the top.

The other man, annoyed with the erroneous descriptions, provided his own, which of course conflicted with all of those previously supplied. He offered the description of something sleek and smooth, like glass or marble, round but curved on the end.

Were they wrong? Or correct but just incomplete?

What is love?

The Bible states that God is love, but our imperfect definition of God only further confuses us in our incomplete definition. Love does not always feel good, and it does not always comfort. In its most raw form, it forces me to stand vulnerable and unprotected. What is love when someone I love and who loves me confronts me with something painful and tells me what I do not want to hear? What is love when love is lost?

What is love? I offer no concrete definition, no delineation of clear description. I offer only advice as another blind man walking the perimeter of an elephant. Feel the facets and open your mind to believe that initial thoughts and previously held notions, while true, do not constitute the whole.

*Amy*

---

- **What is love?**
- **What aspects of love have you experienced?**
- **What aspects do you doubt because you have not experienced them personally?**

## DAY 21

# STEP ONE

"The supreme happiness of life is the conviction that we are loved; loved for ourselves—say rather, loved in spite of ourselves."

—VICTOR HUGO

| Psalm 139 | Luke 7:36-50 | 1 John 4:7-21 |

It was wheat harvesting time in Kansas, and Austin Mann rose early to pick up his grandson, Tracey. They drove twenty miles south of their hometown Quinter to prepare for the long day's work. As they approached the land they were about to harvest, Austin noticed a grain truck approaching, with sixteen-year-old Wesley Miller at the wheel.

"I see that Wayne has taught Wesley how to drive the grain truck," the grandfather said. "I was thinking that you should learn to drive this year."

"But Wesley's much taller and older," protested the twelve-year-old grandson.

"Yes, but your last name is Mann, and his isn't," Austin responded firmly.

The experience branded young Tracey with a confidence that he carried into manhood. It became his right of passage into adulthood. Even to a seat in the US Congress.

Jesus does much the same for us.

"We love, because [Jesus] first loved us," John wrote (1 John 4:19). John became the disciple who debatably understood Jesus' love better than any of the others. He wrote of it prolifically. He received it personally and passed it along generously. Love was branded into his soul because he first received it from Jesus.

In football, the quarterback must hand or pitch the ball to the right guy. If he doesn't, the play is destined for failure. But most fans hardly notice the critical first step: the quarterback must first receive the ball. A single bobbled snap can wreck a drive.

And so it is with love: we must first receive and embrace it.

Try taking a survey of your friends. Ask them, on a scale of 1 to 10, how well they receive love. Few rate themselves better than a four. Keep asking the question, and you'll find an epidemic of insecurity.

Why such dearth of love received?

We carry the shame of our experience, the insecurity of life, the self-perceived ugliness of ourselves. We lose the capacity to see beauty in ourselves, or to imagine the bountiful love and pride that our Maker places upon His children, who were fashioned in His likeness. King David, the adulterer and murderer, grasped it: "For you created my inmost being; you knit me together in my mother's womb. I praise you because I am fearfully and wonderfully made; your works are wonderful, I know that full well" (Psalm 139:13-14 NIV).

And so must we. Step one is to grab onto the Father's love.

*Brad*

---

- What keeps you from receiving your Maker's love?
- Has anyone branded you with love and confidence? Who and how?
- Can you see yourself as "fearfully and wonderfully made"? How?

**DAY 22**

# PERFECTLY IMPERFECT

*"Love is friendship that has caught fire.
It is quiet understanding, mutual confidence, sharing
and forgiving. It is loyalty through good and bad times.
It settles for less than perfection and makes
allowances for human weaknesses."*

—ANN LANDERS

| 1 Corinthians 13:8-10 | John 17:23 | Romans 12:2 |

Perfection is a prison. We start out laboring to reach it but end up in bondage. The perfection we seek is an illusion. But when the true perfect comes, the partial things will fade away. I have strived for perfection my whole life. I know personally how much of a prison this pursuit can become.

Unfortunately, I've also expected the same of my wife and kids. In doing so, I inevitably set them up for failure, because perfection is an unattainable goal. Instead of encouraging them, this expectation ends up hurting our relationship. I'm grateful to the Lord that He has helped them mostly recover from my mistakes.

King David talks about perfection in a very specific context: "The law of the Lord is perfect, restoring the soul" (Psalm 19:7). Seldom do the Scriptures talk about a person being perfect. Rather, the New Testament talks about how wonderfully imperfect we are. The Sermon on the Mount highlights the fact that the Lord fully embraces us despite our imperfection. Jesus says, "Blessed are the poor in spirit, for theirs is the kingdom of heaven" (Matthew 5:3).

There are three words used for *poor* in Greek. Each denotes a certain degree of poverty. The word used in Matthew 5 refers to the poorest of the poor. The Greek word refers to a person who must beg for everything. Instead of rebuking or cursing these people, Jesus turns around and calls them blessed. He takes the people who must beg for what they get and places them in His kingdom. It boggles the mind. It's a counter-cultural phenomenon. Rather than putting the best of the best over His kingdom, God lifts the weakest people with nothing to give. It's His joy to bless them.

When we strive for perfection, it's almost like deciding, "I'm not going to go out unless my hair is perfect. I mean not even one hair out of place!" Of course, this thinking is ridiculous. It keeps us from enjoying the fullness of life. We can never be perfect by earthly or cultural standards. And yet Jesus says, "You are to be perfect, as the heavenly Father is perfect" (Matthew 5:48).

Does this mean we fall short? No, Jesus is saying that we are to be perfect because He is making us perfect in His image. Not here and now, but on a spiritual level, in the eternal perspective. This is a process. And when perfection Himself finally does come, our partial imperfections will be done away.

*Brad*

---

- **When have you thought you needed to be perfect?**
- **Where does striving for perfection leave you?**
- **Who in your life requires you to be perfect?**

## DAY 23

# TUNED IN

"Be clearly aware of the stars and infinity on high.
Then life seems almost enchanted after all."

—VINCENT VAN GOGH

| Isaiah 30:21 | Romans 10:17 | John 10:27 |

We've been told that most communication is nonverbal. Yet our primary means of connection, email and text messaging, eliminate all nonverbal ques (with the exception of emojis). If we're this bad at it, we should ask ourselves, "How good is God at communicating?"

God communicates with us in many ways, including through:

- The Word, His very son, Jesus, and all of His teachings.
- Creation and all the ways that God communicates to us through it, including various plants and animals or examples of human creativity.

- The Holy Spirit, the Teacher who lives inside every believer.
- Other people speaking encouragement into us.
- Our millions of experiences over the course of a lifetime.
- Family and the many experiences therein.
- Writings and teachings.
- Dreams, which can sometimes be vibrant and emotional.

God constantly sends us signals and communications. He is a bit like a tall radio tower, ceaselessly emitting its messages over hundreds of miles and to millions of people. He constantly teaches us truths about life, not the least of which is the height and width and depth and breadth of His great love for us. In fact, I believe He would be satisfied if we simply embraced that notion. Yet God went one step further in creating our capacity to know Him. God promises, "I will put my law in their minds and write it on their hearts" (Jeremiah 31:33, NIV).

How can anything be more personal than that? God Himself writes His law in our minds and on our hearts and walks with us as the Word of the Lord did with the heroes of old. If we want a manual for life, we need look no further than the Scriptures, which were inspired by God Himself and profitable for every important thing we do on Earth.

In answer to the earlier question, I would say that God is pretty good at communicating. He engages every sense. He reminds us who He is every minute. He gets right down to the minutia. His messages never cease. We are permeated by them in every moment.

*Brad*

---

- If God is like that powerful radio tower, then what are you?
- What happens when the radio is mistuned?
- How do you tune in your radio to the right frequency and leave it on, to listen without the distractions of life drawing your attention elsewhere?

# DAY 24

# THE UNGAME

"We the unwilling, led by the unknown, are doing the impossible for the ungrateful. We have done so much, for so long, with so little, we are now qualified to do anything with nothing."

—MOTHER THERESA

| Matthew 9:10-17 | John 14:26-28 | Matthew 5:1-12 |

One day as a kid, my mom came home proudly toting a newly purchased board game. Already an avid competitor in the auspicious realms of Chutes and Ladders, Trouble, and Candyland, my will to win surged at the mere sight of a new family game.

But when my mom revealed her purchase, my competitive drive completely wilted. Instead of a game that I could win, it was a non-game masquerading as a game. A cardboard charlatan, ambiguously dubbed the Ungame. I pouted. I wallowed. I was finally tricked into playing.

The Ungame, as the name suggested, was indeed not a game at all, but rather a litany of questions that prompted discussion between the un-players. A thinly veiled scheme to force fellowship, it was a covert attempt at bonding for the unwitting participants. For the record, there was no record: no score, no points, no plastic crown to wear upon victory. Whatever this Ungame was, I could not find a way to beat it, despite my best efforts. It resisted my understanding. It thwarted my measures of achievement.

Jesus came to a world obsessed with and highly adept at its own game of life. Refusing to play, He brought the Ungame.

He defied the status quo.

From two loaves and a fish, He allowed five thousand to feast. From a motley crew of rabbinical rejects, he trained men to provide the most lasting impact in history. He empowered Peter to walk on water. He turned water into wine. He healed blind men and resurrected dead men.

In the Sermon on the Mount, he spoke paradox and stymied the masses: the poor shall be rich? The weak, strong? The poor in spirit, heirs to the kingdom of God?

These claims and the ways He lived held the rules of the world in contempt. He rendered their game foolish, just as they regarded His game absurd.

Yet, He called us to be a part of what He was doing. He invited us to choose our favorite playing piece and roll the dice of the Ungame.

*Adam*

- What game are you playing?
- What does it mean to join in Jesus' way of life?
- What is the most difficult part of rejecting the world's game?

# DAY 25

# "SAVIOR"

"Be suspicious of anything quick, cheap, or temporary."

—RICHARD FOSTER

| John 3:16-17 | Acts 4:12 | 2 Timothy 1:10 |

Last fall, some friends and I attended a concert after work. One of those friends introduced me to his colleague, a Capitol Hill staffer new to the District.

"Why did you come to DC?" I asked her.

"God," she said.

"God? God brought you to DC?"

"Yes. He said 'no' to everything else and led me here."

"What do you think about Jesus?" I asked.

"He's my Lord and Savior."

The conversation did not come to a whiplash-inducing halt. We spoke a little longer about various other topics, but as I walked away from this exchange, one thing stuck with me: Savior. What does that mean? What does that mean for most people who say this? What does this mean for her? For me?

We've used this definition for so long that we've lost our ability to describe what it means.

The word itself, since becoming part of our script, has even lost some of its teeth. Yes, the theological, doctrinal statements about saving are vital, and they deserve much thought. But perhaps there's more to Jesus' saving than we've mentioned.

From what does He save? Sin? Our wrongdoing and wrong thinking? That's what I hear, but it's never seemed satisfactory. He pays the price for wrongs and failures. But which wrongs and failures? Has He pulled me out of them? If so, why do I still struggle with them? Were they killing me? Did I realize it? I mulled this over for the entire forty-five-minute car ride home that night.

Today, those questions still weigh on me as I look at my day. Today, I'll see coworkers, customers, and roommates. I'll talk to family. I'll work all day, and I'll encounter unexpected people and events bumping into my agenda. I'll need to relate to them.

I'll need saving in all encounters. Saving from myself, my failures, my agenda. These do kill me as I attempt to love others. These often impede my ability to give to, care for, and help others. Jesus says to love others as yourself. Well, I can't. All my stuff gets in the way. That must qualify as some sort of sin or wrong or failure.

I have all these small but subversive addictions, fears, false dreams. I operate with a great deal of stubbornness and pride. If left alone, they'll rule over me. If given to Jesus, He says He can teach me a better way, set me free. But it's not a one-and-done deal. It's more of a day-by-day, moment-by-moment process.

Fortunately, the author of our faith is also the perfector (see Hebrews 12:2), working with us, shaping us, displaying patience and extravagant forgiveness for our many stumbles and falls.

A savior by definition saves. I need saving all the time. The saving Jesus does, in all of its manifold forms, I need every day, every moment.

*Adam*

---

- **From what do you need saving?**
- **From what has Jesus saved you?**
- **To what extent do you still recognize the need for saving today?**

**DAY 26**

# A MAN-MADE GOD

"Religion is regarded by the common people as true, by the wise as false, and by the rulers as useful."

—SENECA

| James 1:27 | Acts 11:26 | 1 Peter 4:16 |

Search the Scriptures and see if you can find it anywhere. You know, the *C* word. Don't know what I'm talking about? "Christian." People use the word often, seldom considering its many meanings. As we talk with others, we find a multitude of definitions.

To the Muslim, it means the other religion.
To the atheist, it is the enemy.
To the Eastern, it means Western.
To the developing world, it means capitalist.
To the Catholic, it means Catholic.
To the evangelical, it means only those who are saved. (As if we can really know if another person is saved.)
To the non-evangelical, it means the club to which he or she will never be admitted.

Yet we find rare references to it in the Scriptures. Only three. Two are clearly spoken by church outsiders (see Acts 11:26, Acts 26:28), and one is in reference to a category of people persecuted by the Romans (see 1 Peter 4:16).

Jesus never uttered the word, as far as we know. If Jesus' immediate followers had been asked what the word meant, they would have had no basis for a definition.

It's a word that first took form among the Jewish-Roman persecutors of the Way. In the fourth century the Roman Emperor Constantine the Great ordained Christianity as the official church of Rome. He promptly saddled the new church with pagan alliances from his own pagan past. Yet this new church was the work of man. He fashioned it with his hands and called it good. Though many worshipped the Lord with a pure heart in its sanctuaries, this new religion exalted a man-made god. We should not call Jesus the founder of this "religion." He never intended to found a new religion. In fact, "pure and undefiled religion" is caring for orphans and widows (James 1:27). It's not an orthodoxy but selflessness.

Don't look for any help from the Apostle Paul either. He said all believing Gentiles were grafted into the Jewish heritage. Both Paul and Jesus never intended to depart from the Jewish faith, as far as we can tell. They would find it absurd that their followers would fixate on constructing a new religion.

Jesus rejected man's attempt to invent religion. He referred to religion as wineskins that could not hold new wine. Jesus rejected worldly religious clout. He came. He loved. He related to others.

*Brad*

- What does the word "Christian" mean to you?
- Does it feel like an inclusive or exclusive word? To what extent was Jesus exclusive or inclusive?
- How does Jesus refer to his followers? Why?

# DAY 27

# WHAT HE'S SAYING

*"I want to talk to my son! I don't care what it costs, I don't care what the stupid doctors say is right or wrong. I want to talk to my son!"*

—FROM MR. HOLLAND'S OPUS

| John 5:36-39 | Jeremiah 31:31-34 | Luke 24:25-27 |

College entrance essays ask which historical figures you would like to meet. Magazine reporters ask which three people you'd like to have for dinner.

We envision our discussions with these people, brooding over the grand questions we'd ask. Why did the Beatles break up? Why did Barry Sanders retire so soon? What was T. S. Eliot trying to convey with the *Wasteland*?

We each carry a massive collection of these queries for God.

Why war? Why poverty? Why disease?

Are You not good? Are You not loving? Are You not powerful?

Why don't You fix this mess? Fix my life? Fix my heart?

The questions linger. Then we encounter a teacher, someone with the answers. He or she dumps the proverbial truckload of information on us, and so much of the murkiness becomes clear. Consequently, our tutor renders him or herself obsolete. Now that our questions are answered, this person isn't so interesting. We just wanted the information, not a relationship.

We sought easy answers and quick information, and we came upon an individual replete with vast experience. The realization arrives: this person just might have something else to say, something about which I've never had a question. This person might have something to offer that I can't imagine. Perhaps this person will have something of him or herself to give.

Now turn the scenario around. When someone seeks nothing but information from us, we wonder, "Is that all you want? Just this commodity? Do you not want to know me? I can give you more of myself."

Parents know this feeling well. God knows it well also.

He also knows our questions remain, even though we don't fully understand what answers we need. Or, more important, we haven't yet pondered the deeper questions.

What can He give as a response? Can He provide an answer as complicated and deep as we need, given the harsh, brutal, and complex experiences of life?

He does. He presents His answer in the only understandable form: a person. He offers not a word or a bullet-point doctrine, but a person. We want to know this person, and we want this person to know us. In light of the world's dizzying questions, the only answer we truly need is in the form of a human.

Jesus walked into the world. Isn't that what we always wanted?

*Adam*

---

- **Who, then, is Jesus? What does God tell me through Him?**
- **What is the message of Jesus?**
- **Why is this important?**

# DAY 28

# JESUS THROUGH THE CRACKS

"The wife of a rural pastor would seem to have little reason for smiling. She and her husband lost their oldest son when he was nine. They are poor and have no visible hope of ever moving out of poverty. The needs of their church and community demand their time, their energy, their resources."

—MAHATMA GANDHI

| Luke 6:20-23 | Psalm 84:5 | James 1:9-12 |

When she opened the door to her home, ushering in visitors, she laughed warmly, smiled authentically. She felt glad to receive guests. She quickly prepared a meal, set it before them, and asked nothing in return. When told "thank you," she smiled again, revealing a broken front tooth, another mark of a hard life.

Her guests pitied her for this. They pitied her poverty, her hard life, her lack of sophistication. But she smiled still. And soon these guests realized how much wealth she truly possessed. Peace belonged to her. Strength to serve belonged to her. Joy belonged to her. And all she had she set before her guests.

Her guests, two young, upper middle-class American young men had seen little and lived less. They knew Jesus only in sermons and pop-religion books. Now they saw Him in the broken-toothed woman they pitied. She'd met Jesus in the pain and hardness of life that breaks one's teeth and thus creates space for Him to smile through.

This broken tooth represented the price she'd gladly paid for living. She'd been chipped in the process of life, and the accoutrements of Madison Avenue or Rodeo Drive wouldn't mask these manifestations. She had a little more room for Jesus, and as she opened the door to her home, He appeared with her. When she served the food, He sat down to dine with the guests. When she smiled, He embraced the recipients.

The boys had only to see her, to look on her, to see Jesus. He changed their skewed view of beauty to teach them that He resided there, and that they were the ones to be pitied. For they, with their unchipped teeth and unworn bodies, had lived little and loved less. But He loved them through this broken tooth, this willing life of a pastor's wife. They, in turn, received His love as they witnessed its stunning transformative power. What they'd thought on the margins of beauty had begun to appear gorgeous in their eyes.

They saw her beauty because they saw Him in her, with her.

He shone through her because she held room inside of herself for Him. Her broken tooth, her broken life, her hard days, and many trials had created a place for Jesus. She had allowed Him to shine through as she lived a life poured out.

Even in her pain and sadness and struggles, she had much to smile about. She, above all women, was blessed.

*Adam*

---

- Do you look for Jesus in the hard places? When or where?
- To what extent do you recognize that He works through the hard and broken parts of your life?
- How does seeing Jesus in those places and in other people change your perspective?
- Try looking for Him in the strangers you pass today. Try looking for Him in your friends, family, colleagues, and even in your enemies.

# DAY 29

# ROLES OF JESUS

Keating [standing on his desk]: Why do I stand up here?
Dalton: To feel taller!
Keating: No! [dings a bell with his foot]: Thank you for playing Mr. Dalton. I stand upon my desk to remind myself that we must constantly look at things in a different way.
—DEAD POET'S SOCIETY

1 Corinthians 9:19-23 | Luke 9:18-20

Teacher. Rabbi. Messiah. King. Savior. Redeemer. Friend. Christ. Servant. Son. Prophet. Man. God. Rebel. Revolutionary. Priest. Intercessor.

The roles of Jesus. All true.

But what if I don't see them all? What if I believe in Him but only one part of Him? Or in only three parts of Him? What if I love Jesus the man? Will He accept that love? What if I follow Jesus the rabbi? Does that meet His command to "Learn of me" (Matthew 11:29)? What if I believe in the teacher? Is that faith sufficient?

What part of Jesus is the integral part? What role is the right role? Which must I believe in?

Is it enough to see Him as Savior even if I cannot see Him as teacher or man? What if I see Him as prophet and revolutionary but do not see Him yet as Messiah? Is that sufficient?

Who claims the right to determine how we must view Jesus to be acceptable to Him? Have we taught "as doctrines the precepts of men" (Matthew 15:9)?

Did His words, "I am the way, and the truth, and the life; no one comes to the Father but through Me" (John 14:6), define how we come through Him? Did those words tell us how to understand His way, to grasp the truth, to live the life?

We don't like the Jesus others see if they see something we don't or only see one facet of His person. We say, "That's not enough," and they must believe these ten points about Jesus, or they can't follow or believe. "You're out!" we yell.

Does anyone really see all of Jesus?

Furthermore, does anyone love all of Jesus? The very hard parts? His teachings, for instance. When they call us to die, do we really love and believe in that? Do we embrace the Savior but reject the one calling to die?

We must see Jesus as fully as possible, but we cannot dictate what of Jesus others must see. He didn't grant us this authority. When asked if many were being saved, Jesus said, "Strive to enter through the narrow door" (Luke 13:24), essentially saying, "Don't worry about others. Worry about you."

If we see Him, we've begun looking at the truth. Maybe we don't see all of it, but we see enough to move forward. He'll instruct us. And perhaps we can learn from each other about Jesus. The Lord. The rabbi. The teacher. The rebel and revolutionary. The man. The King. The friend. The redeemer. The son. The person.

*Adam*

---

- What in your mind is the principal role of Jesus? Why do you think this?
- What other roles do other people see Jesus playing?
- Why do you think certain roles are more important than others?
- How did Jesus identify Himself, and what roles did He emphasize?
- How does seeing Jesus differently equate to seeing all of Him?

# DAY 30

# GOD CREATIVE

"It is the creative potential itself in human beings that is the image of God."

—MARY DALY

| Psalm 33:6 | John 1:1-14 | Colossians 1:15-20 |

People try to escape Jesus for as long as they can. We can ignore Him, and we do. We develop systems: financial, social, and especially spiritual, to get away from needing or heeding Him. Loving us, He's jealous; but loving us, He doesn't force us to reciprocate.

Still, we have trouble escaping Him. Maybe we can't because we look like Him. We were made through Him. My friends, family, and even my enemies were all fashioned and designed to be like Him, so I find His picture everywhere. His nature is to be in relationship, to be known, to love something so much and we see that in ourselves.

Paul said everything exists for Jesus and that everything is held together in and through Him. Yeats said, "The centre cannot hold." It appears so, given how fast and loose we play life. But He didn't understand who holds the shaky center.

Every person bears the image of Jesus. This fact conjures up something like the word *holy* with everyone we meet. We deal with images of Jesus all the time, even those who are difficult. We curse these people, sometimes with His name, no less.

We try to escape Him, yet He has shown Himself to be more than creative; He's shown Himself to be ingenious, enterprising. This is because He's a lover, jealous but not forceful.

He shows up looking like us. Now people run into Him on the streets or in bookstores or warehouses or at dinner parties. Because He has shown up.

Still, we run away.

God created us through Jesus. So, even now Jesus continues to create when He meets us. He reveals to us wild and alien things, thoughts like new colors. They come from another place, and we've neither heard nor seen them before. We don't understand them, just as we don't understand Him. They recreate broken people, broken relationships, and a broken world. They make us look more like this wild and uncontainable Jesus.

We were each made to be the kind of person Jesus is.

Everyone we'll ever meet was made to be the kind of person Jesus is. And they were made for Him.

Jesus hasn't finished creating. He did something beautiful the first go-round. And we broke it. Now He wants to make it new, to make it better. Do we want to escape that?

*Adam*

- When do you want to get away from Jesus? Why?
- When have you met anyone who resembled Him? What was this person like?
- Do you believe Jesus' teachings make us new creatures? Is this a good thing?

# DAY 31

# THE PURPOSE-DRIVEN WORD

"Lord, I flinch and pray, send thy necessity."

—WENDELL BERRY

| Isaiah 55:1-13 (esp. 7-11) | 1 Corinthians 1:18-31 | Jeremiah 9:23-24 |

A few things to keep in mind: (1) we don't understand what Jesus is doing; but (2) we think we do; (3) He knows what He's doing; and (4) He'll accomplish His Father's purposes despite us.

Let's start with history. In the desert, the Hebrews couldn't see the promised land, but God did. He got them there, even though they thought He'd lost His mind.

When Jesus showed up, the Jews expected a messiah of a different sort. He wasn't William Wallace. Where was their MacArthur or Patton? Jesus confounded his disciples. They spent three years with Him, day and night, and they understood what He was teaching only after He returned from the tomb.

Men of every age tend to privilege their historical vantage point: "We've seen the past, and we've risen above it. We're more civilized. We possess greater understanding, and we've evolved. We won't botch it as our ancestors did."

If we learn anything, let us learn that we don't know everything. We don't see it all. To think we do stifles our learning. We paint our own caricature of Jesus, and we miss Him when He doesn't match it exactly. He seldom does.

Yet we still think we can contain Him, His ways, and His plans, in our pocket. We think we know what's best for the Middle East, and we certainly assume we know where He stands on that issue. We're certain we know when He'll show up again, though He said that even He doesn't know. We certainly know His politics, right?

The story of the twelve replays itself in our lives. We betray Him as Judas did, misunderstand His values as James and John did, and deny Him as Peter did. Our puny minds have no idea about the experiences of others, especially from centuries ago and cultures far removed from our own. Let us not presume to know God's ways and thoughts. Let's not lose hope, either. Jesus worked with the twelve. He didn't give up but kept teaching them. He kept working with those men, who stumbled every day. He focused on a purpose with them, and He does with us.

His Father sent Him with a job to do, and He doesn't plan to go home without seeing it through.

*Adam*

- To what extent do you believe there's mystery inherent in God?
- Have your ways, even those you thought were His, ever conflicted with His? How did you respond?
- What, if anything, does Jesus say that startles you? What and why?

# DAY 32

# ALL THE TIME

"You were always on my mind."

—WILLIE NELSON

| Matthew 28:16-20 | Luke 24:13-32 | John 5:36-40 |

It looks so obvious in retrospect. He sent us pictures all along. The pictures showed us what He looked like. That way we might recognize Him when we meet Him.

He said, "Let there be light." Jesus said, "I am the light" (John 9:5)

He gave manna, the bread of angels, in the desert trek from Egypt. Jesus said, "I am the bread of life." He then said bread alone is insufficient for life; we need every word He utters. John says, "The Word became flesh" (John 1:14).

Moses struck a rock in the desert, and it gave his people water. Jesus said, I "would have given you the living water" (John 4:10).

His people asked for a king. Jesus said, "I am a king" (John 18:37). And Paul said, "Everyone will kneel before Him." David said, "The Lord is my shepherd." Jesus said, "I am the good shepherd" (John 10:11).

The people had judges before they had kings. Jesus said, the Father "has given all judgment to" the Son (John 5:22). He gave the people priests to pray for them. The writer of Hebrews called Jesus the high priest who prays for us (see Hebrews 7:25).

His people would place their sins on a goat and send the goat into the wilderness to take the sins away. John the Baptist called Him, "The lamb who takes away the sins of the world" (John 1:29). His people had cities of refuge, and they called God "their place of rest" (Psalm 90). Jesus said, "Come to Me, and I'll give you rest" (Matthew 11:28).

Solomon spoke to his bride. In the upper room, Jesus spoke to his friends, promising as the bridegroom to "come to [them]" (John 14:28).

Jacob saw a ladder connecting heaven and earth. Jesus said, the way to the Father was through Me (see John 14:6).

Jeremiah said God's word felt like fire in his heart, in his bones, even. Jesus said He came to start a fire (see Luke 12:49).

God told Moses his name is "I AM" (Exodus 3:14). Jesus said before Abraham was born, "I AM" (John 8:58).

Jesus told the Jews they kept looking for answers to life in the book. But the book points to Him (see John 5:39). The book sends pictures of Him; it does not function as a file of projects to complete before folks go home at the end of life. Did they not see the pictures in the envelope?

We keep looking for the way to real life, to the good life. The path leading there doesn't run through a method, but instead through a Man.

Jesus said, "I am the way, and the truth, and the life" (John 14:6).

*Adam*

---

- Do you look for the things to do or the person to know? Why?
- What happens when you focus on the pictures in the text and in your life?
- How will your world begin to look different?

## DAY 33

# WHO?

*"Giving names to things is a way of knowing them and seeing them as well."*

—ALLEN LACEY

| John 1:1-5 | Genesis 17:1 | Genesis 28:3 |

I heard this in a class once. Researchers showed a battery of images to individuals with one eye covered. If the individuals knew a word for the object flashed before their eyes, they could remember it. If they didn't have a word for the object, they didn't remember it.

The researchers concluded that people need a name to know.

"In the beginning was the Word" (John 1:1).

God gave us names to know Him and His actions.

From Genesis to Malachi, God is referred to as *Yahweh*, the self-existent one, I Am Who I Am, nearly seven thousand times.

He is *El*, mighty (Genesis 28:3). He drives out nations before His people. He says He is *El Shaddai* (Genesis 17:1), the entirely sufficient One. He provides old man Abraham with a son. Paul recounts Jesus telling him, "My grace is sufficient for you" (2 Corinthians 12:9).

Moses calls Him *Adonai*, Master (Exodus 4:10). God orders Moses to act as He desires, and Jesus commands wind and waves to act as He wishes. Abraham calls Him *Yahweh Jireh*, God the Provider (Genesis 22:14). He sends manna to the Hebrews in the desert, and Jesus provides food for five thousand.

God says He is the Healer, *Yahweh-Rophe* (Exodus 15:22-26). He heals a widow's son through Elijah. Jesus heals lepers, restores sight to the blind, and sends the lame out walking. David says the Lord is Judge (Psalm 9:8), and God says judgment belongs to Him alone (Genesis 18:25). Jesus says God gave Him judgment (John 5:22).

Moses called Him *Zur*, or Rock (Deuteronomy 32:18). Jesus said His teachings are a foundation like rock for a person's life (Matthew 7:24).

Gideon says the Lord is Peace, calling Him *Yahweh Shalom* (Judges 6:24) after the Lord promises it in verse 23. Jesus gives the disciples His peace (John 14:27).

David calls Him *Eyaluth*, his strength (Psalm 22:19). Jesus told Paul, "My strength is made perfect in weakness" (2 Corinthians 12:9, KJV).

Hagar called God, *El Roi*, the One Who Sees (Genesis 16:13), because He saw her sadness. Jesus told Nathanael He saw him under a fig tree, far away (John 1:48).

Isaiah says God's sign will be one whose name is Immanuel, God with us (Isaiah 7:14). Jesus said, "I am with you always" (Matthew 28:20).

*Adam*

- What do you call Jesus?
- How do you know Him in experience?
- What do His names mean to you?

## DAY 34

# IS JESUS ENOUGH FOR ME?

"I think the apostle James answered that in the first council in Jerusalem when he said that God's purpose for this age is to call out a people for his name. That is what God is doing today. He is calling people out of the world for his name, whether they come from the Muslim world, the Buddhist world, the Christian world or the non-believing world. They are members of the body of Christ because they have been called by God."

—BILLY GRAHAM

Matthew 7:21-27  |  John 12:27-36 (esp. 32)  |  Colossians 1:15-20 (esp. 20)

Is Jesus enough? Is He enough to bring us together, even if you're Protestant and I'm Catholic? Or if I'm Tutsi and you're Hutu? Perhaps we're both conservatives? Is He enough to bring us together without making us copies of one another?

Is it okay for us to disagree on cosmetic surgery, women priests, politics, evolution, worship styles, Bible translations, or the Israel-Palestine conflict? Do we need to share the same views on home schooling, homosexuality, and abortion? Do we both need to condemn Harry Potter or celebrate Trinity Broadcasting Network? Can we think differently about the end times and the Left Behind series?

Is Jesus enough? Can He really bring to Himself every tribe, tongue, nation, and creed? Is He big enough to cross boundaries of race, age, class, nationality, economics, politics, culture, background, lifestyle, sins, doctrine, and religion? Can Jesus overcome all of that?

Will we go to Jesus for answers? Will we pursue those different from us with love? Will we live from an ethic of love when it means embracing what we cannot understand? When rebuking? Will we live on issues or on a person's teachings?

Before you say, "yes," think about what your yes really means. Does it mean, "Yes, somehow, against my lack of belief, Jesus can place a bridge of love in the space between us"? Or does it really mean, "If by some miracle you come over to my side, agree with me, act in a manner I approve, and live accordingly, then, yes, we can get along"? Must I adhere to your five points? Is it enough I want to follow Jesus? Or have an interest in Him? Must I follow your laws you say are the Bible's in order to be your friend?

Are the teachings of Jesus authoritative enough for us to try to live out? Even if everything about us diverges? Maybe we need those teachings because everything diverges. Is His life's example sufficient evidence that He wants us to figure out how to care about each other?

Did His death conquer death but not the prejudices we hold? Could He die so that we can judge and exclude each other? Or was it enough to convince us to begin reaching toward Him, and in doing so, toward one another?

Is He enough?

*Adam*

---

- What is unity?
- How does Jesus unite?
- How do you, with His help, bring down division?
- Is Jesus enough for you?

# DAY 35

# SPOKEN

*"No matter what anybody tells you, words and ideas can change the world."*

—JOHN KEATING
TO HIS STUDENTS IN DEAD POETS' SOCIETY

| Genesis 1 | Luke 5:12-26 | Hebrews 4:12-13 |

God spoke. He said, "Let there be light," and light appeared. He said, "Let us make man," and man was created.

Jesus spoke. Whenever the gospels record Jesus healing an individual, Jesus speaks before the healing occurs. The same holds true for His calming wild winds, feeding thousands, turning water into wine, and even His death and resurrection.

It should amaze us that God's very words bring about their intention. He says, "Let this be so," and it is. Jesus says, "You are well," and you are. He says, "Come out from the grave," and a man steps through the door of mortality.

When Jesus tells a common thief dying in a public execution, "Today, you shall be with Me in paradise" (Luke

23:43), He speaks the truth. When He says, "Your sins are forgiven," we can believe Him. He has such an authority that His very words change physical and spiritual states. Those who witnessed Him in action recognized His authority.

The miracles themselves—the healings, the stilling of storms, the feasts He provided, His rising from death—might all hold a secondary purpose. He saw blind and crippled men and wanted to restore them; He saw nature in need of control; He saw families wanting for food; and He saw a need to deal with death. But He needed us to believe His ability to restore our lives and souls, to calm hearts in turmoil, to feed our spirits, to restore us from the living dead into the living living.

If He can accomplish these things in His life, we can believe Him when He speaks into our lives. He told us we're blessed when we think we're cursed (see Matt. 5:1-12); He told us we're forgiven when we think we've exceeded grace's grasp; He told us the kingdom is at hand; He told us He wouldn't leave us alone; He said that He's with us and that He'd never leave.

His healing of bodies foreshadowed the greater healing of persons. He could make the body right, and so He could make the person right.

"Which is easier, to say, 'Your sins are forgiven,' or to say, 'Get up and walk'? But so that you may know the Son of Man has authority on earth to forgive sins" (Matthew 9:5-6).

Healing a broken body might be easier to believe. That's why He started there.

*Adam*

- Jesus says we find life in Him. Do you believe this? Why or why not?
- To what extent does God confer value on you because He has spoken to you directly?
- How do you see the physical representing the spiritual?

# PRAYER

# DAY 36

# BLESS GOD'S HEART

*"Spiritual lust: going to God to get something from him instead of going to him just to be with him."*

—OSWALD CHAMBERS

| Genesis 5:22-24 | Exodus 33:9-11 | John 15:14-15 |

I prayed this morning. No, I didn't quite pray; I unloaded. Some people have those deep prayers where they sit and listen for God. The late Mother Teresa, when asked what she said when she prayed, replied, "Nothing. I just listen." When asked what God said, she replied, "Nothing. He just listens too."

That's beyond me.

My method: pour everything out on God for some cathartic relief.

Praise? I don't really do that. I spend so much time telling God all my needs that I can't remember His goodness for listening to all my selfish requests.

Thanks? I'll do that a few times. In the midst of, "Bless so and so," I sometimes feel a bright gratitude for some loved one and then I offer up an affectionate but inadequate, "Thank you so much for this person," because that's all I can muster in the midst of my joy and poorly prayed prayers.

I ask and then I ask some more. And I keep asking. Please bless this person. Please fix this in me. Please heal this situation. Please make this person strong. Please tell this person who they really are. Please draw this person to you. Please bless me. Please bless her. Please bless him.

Sometimes I write my prayers down. This please blessings occupied about two and a half journal pages. Somewhere, somehow, a new thought arrived, and it opened my mind for the day. Despite its subtle onset it was revolutionary.

How might I bless God? Might just approaching God to be near Him make Him feel blessed? Might giving to Him of myself be the blessing I can confer?

A scene in the film *Bruce Almighty* illustrates this desire of God. Bruce, played by Jim Carrey, asks God, "How can you make someone love you without affecting free will?"

God replies, "Welcome to my world, son. If you come up with an answer on that one, let me know." In the midst of all I desire and need, perhaps all He desires is my love.

Jesus tells us we're His friends, and God spoke to Moses as a man speaks to his friend. God walked with Adam in the garden, and He had a close friendship with Enoch. God wants to be friends with us. That's what the Scriptures and the teachings of Jesus tell us. If we're friends, I need to pull up a chair to this table of friendship. Instead, I typically just drop a request in the comment box. Actually, I drop about fifty a day, and I don't offer up any . . . offers. I never sit down with God and talk to Him about life or His problems. I certainly don't ask, "What can I do for You today?" I neither spend time getting to be His friend nor looking to care for Him.

I make God out to be a blessing fairy. I use God. I mistreat Him.

Still, He waits in hope that I will learn what it means to be a friend. Still, He waits for me to mature into the sort of person who will spend time with Him, who will listen, who will wait and then offer my heart and my hands. Finally, when I do mature into a friend, God will be blessed by me.

*Amy*

---

- How often do you listen to God's heart?
- How often do you think about what matters to God?
- To what extent do you consider Him a friend?

# DAY 37

# VOLUNTARY VERSUS INVOLUNTARY PRAYER

*"If you are lonely when you're alone, you are in bad company."*

—JEAN-PAUL SARTRE

| Psalm 63:6 | Lamentations 2:19 | James 4:8 |

Along with a group of friends this morning, we discussed what exactly drives us toward prayer. We are all spiritual men, who share the plight of distraction. We all agreed that nothing drives us toward prayer more than pain. Whether we are dragged into prayer by emotional suffering, heartache, health issues, financial hardship, alienation, or isolation, they have brought us to our knees. But is there another way?

As I pondered this question, an answer popped into my head. I wondered, *Is there a way to be drawn to prayer, as opposed to being driven into it like cattle?* Immediately a word came to me: *solitude*.

As a twenty-first-century American, I am shackled by urgency. Whether minor emergencies are real or perceived, I dart to and fro, putting out the flames of these petty urgencies. From what I can tell, my friends suffer from the same problem.

Short of checking myself into a monastery, I wondered how I could create solitude in my own effort to be drawn into prayer by something positive. *Is it possible*, I wondered, *that I could enjoy solitude so much as to be drawn to prayer on a regular basis?*

My thoughts turned to the early days of my faith, during which I needed no outside stimulus to provoke me to pray. I remember being drawn in like a lover to a love note from Him. I would go to my quiet place almost every day. The experience was like having an appointment with the Almighty Himself.

Just thinking about that period of life fills me with envy. In our hearts, we want to go back. If we could just turn back the clock. We should, and we will.

*Brad*

---

- **Where and when do you find solitude?**
- **How can solitude help you grow?**
- **Is there any way you could treat this more like an appointment with the One who loves you?**

# DAY 38

# INCOHERENCE TO ARTICULACY

"But it's sure nice talking to you, Dad.
It's been sure nice talking to you."

—HARRY CHAPIN,
"CAT'S IN THE CRADLE"

| Matthew 6:5-15 | Mark 1:35-39 | Luke 6:12 |

We learned incorrectly. We assumed that we needed to begin with perfection instead of traveling along the continuum of life as a journey. Communication takes place in progression. We age. We grow. We develop in thinking and faith, ultimately learning the desire to learn how to listen. And learning the desire to learn how to pray.

Our life reflects the movements of our spirit:

*Infancy*: We enter into this world. Our relationship with our parents stems from our state of constant need and incapability. Communication consists of a series of whimpers and wails during the day and throughout the night. We are hungry. We are tired. Feed us. Clothe us. Put us to bed.

*Toddlerhood*: Our crying slowly transforms into language. Along the way, parents call it gibberish. Every kid's dialect proves rather unique and decipherable only by the parents who provide interpretation for friends, grandparents, and bewildered babysitters. We learn language but continually befuddle others and muddle expressions. We attempt and fail, but our parents delight in the small steps of sophistication.

*Childhood*: Broken sentences transform into coherent speech, thanks to patient parents and *Sesame Street*. Our approach changes with maturity, but our premise remains. I want the candy at the store. I want the new toy at the mall. I want to stay up later and watch one more show. I don't want to eat vegetables.

*Adolescence*: Our minds attempt increased complexity, and our deviousness develops. "I want" turns to "I need." "I need" turns to "I'm gonna take" and "I'm going." We demand things from our parents, most vehemently our right to ourselves. We grow up and discover independence, or at least the illusion of it. We find "our way" and vow to be controlled by no one.

*Adulthood* (hopefully): We chose our path. We learned. Some chose the hard way. Some chose a path of less resistance. We know the power of words. We realize that they enable relationship and that our parents want one. We realize they want dialogue, conversation, and a friendship. We grow into the reality that they have lives and feelings that they want to share.

Revolutionary.

*Amy*

- What inhibits you from communicating with God?
- What is prayer to you?
- How can you pursue a deeper level of communication with God?

**DAY 39**

# ALONE?
# OR HOW TO LISTEN

*"The first duty of love is to listen."*

—PAUL TILLICH

| Jeremiah 29:11-14 | Romans 10:17 | Luke 6:12-19 |

We struggle with the concept of listening. This stems from our inability to value silence, to seek out solitude. We fill every moment and space with sound. Coffee shops, bookstores, and bars hum with music, as streets and cities buzz with urban life's song: construction, transportation, communication. Runners often carry one indispensable accessory in addition to shoes: some form of earpiece. Commercial gyms without music or televisions don't exist.

Given this penchant for sound, one might think we listen well. Actually, we are easily distracted. And there's a difference.

Now remove a modern person from such an environment. Remove yourself. The adaptation to the sound of only waves on sand takes more than a moment. The silence and solitude appear so alien. The change of pace feels confining.

We avoid it. We don't want to hear, to listen. Oh, we say we do, but we choose the sounds of civilization—music and 24/7 news—instead. Maybe the sounds that flood over us stave off the loneliness. Maybe these sounds drown out the questions within us.

To listen, to hear from God, we must leave the crowds, the crush of sound and noise. We need to be alone to empty our lives of inconsequential distraction. It'll take a moment to adjust to the stillness, maybe a while.

It'll take a few more moments to empty our heads of the inner discussions, all the lists we extend, all the worries and fears and insecurities about ourselves. Perhaps just telling God all these things will purge us and allow us to begin listening.

This rarely happens in a social setting. We learn this alone, in silence, and in solitude. That's where we can begin finding one who waits for us. He doesn't want a place on our checklist. He wants to be the list, the conversation, the one with whom we desire to speak.

*Adam*

---

▫ **What distracts you during prayer?**

▫ **Is it hard for you to listen? Why or why not?**

▫ **What prevents you from seeking out real solitude with God?**

# DAY 40

# OWNING THE RELATIONSHIP

*"I want you to want me."*

—CHEAP TRICK

| Daniel 9 | 1 Kings 19:9-14 | 1 Timothy 2:1-8 |

I wait by the phone. I continually check my email. Will anybody call first? Write first? Or make first contact? When people tell me to just stop by their houses, do I? Or do I resist and refrain out of myriad excuses. They spoke without sincerity. Why should I inconvenience them?

Doubt restrains me. I fail to recognize the validity, power, and beauty of simple presence.

I remember walking the dusty streets of northern Uganda. The days passed slowly. I transitioned from the self-imposed busy bustle of America to the unscheduled, relationally timed pace of the Africans. I spent two or three days with a group of mentors and a houseful of children in their care. From my stringently high, action-based standards I did not do anything.

We sat. We talked. We sat. We sat in silence. We chewed sugar cane. We played games. We helped make dinner. We sat some more.

They served—continually. Heaping plates of warm meals appeared before me before they ate. They asked me to share my life. They honored me by giving the time and arena to speak. As I prepared to leave, they asked to pray for me, blessing me immensely. I felt undeserving.

Walking away from that house, I expressed my feelings of inadequacy to a friend who now lives in Uganda. She understood but challenged me to abandon the merit-based confines I so inherently believed. She told me to put myself into the worn sandals of those village children. Of all the continents in the world, I came to Africa. Of all the countries in Africa, I came to Uganda. Of all the regions in Uganda, I came to Gulu. And, of all the innumerable huts, houses, and mud-caked shacks dotting the barren landscape, I came to their home and ate with them. It was an honor and a privilege that proved inexplicably mutual.

I still try to translate this perspective into life here in the United States. I attempt to just show up instead of waiting for the other to initiate. I try to call first and call back when voicemails are not returned. I vow to send emails, letters, and care packages just because.

What about my relationship with God? I treat Him as I do my parents. I respond after they initiate. I don't make the effort to show up or exist intentionally. I simply coexist.

What if the inverse occurred? What if I invited my parents out for dinner? What if I made the pot of coffee, poured some cups, and sat down asking about their lives. I could. You could. We retain the option.

What would happen if the inverse occurred with God? What if I acted instead of reacted? What if I initiated conversation simply to be with Him, not expecting to receive? What if I believed that He yearned to spend the day, the hour, the minute with me?

I am the one who is busy.

*Amy*

---

- **When do you initiate with other people?**
- **When do you initiate with God?**
- **What are you afraid of?**

# DAY 41

# CONSTANTLY

"I pray because I can't help myself. I pray because the need flows out of me all the time, waking and sleeping."

—ANTHONY HOPKINS
AS C. S. LEWIS IN THE SHADOWLANDS

| Luke 18:1-8 | 1 Thessalonians 5:16-18 | Proverbs 3:5-6 |

What a toll modern technology takes on interaction. A new generation craves the next text message and rarely writes a personal note on paper. And now we have video conferencing. Soon, we'll make face-to-face communication obsolete.

Cell phones might possess some level of redemption. Yes, they represent inherent interruption. You speak with someone or meet with someone, and the phone inserts itself into the situation. Cellularity does offer us greater access to one another, though. This can be good. We become increasingly available. While some of the cell phone world deserves elimination, the fact that we can, if absolutely necessary, reach another person, is cause for celebration.

The human desire is to connect, and we find some empowerment in these technologies.

God created us to connect with Him. Yet, all too often, we relegate our time with Him to an hour a week, or maybe token nods at meals or monologues we call prayer at night.

Yet Jesus' life and teachings tell us God wants to communicate with us all the time. Like a parent hearing his or her kid explain in detail his new toy, God wants to hear about what excites us.

The lines are open. The Lord listens. The Lord speaks. What makes us think we should wait for a five-minute window before bed to present to Him our thoughts, requests, and concerns? Why should He have to wait until then to speak? Why should He be forced to wait until Saturday afternoon or Sunday morning to tell you what's on His mind?

The engaging God urges us to speak and listen. He doesn't have a to-do list of people to call each day; rather, He waits to speak to and hear from every person.

The shocking nature of this reality should compel us to speak with Him daily, even hourly. We should ask and look to receive, knock and wait for the door to open, seek and know we'll find. Because He waits.

*Adam*

---

- How often do you pray? Why not more often?
- Do you marvel that God listens to you?
- Is it possible to "pray without ceasing" (1 Thessalonians 5:17)? Why or why not?

## DAY 42

# GENIE OR JESUS?

"Your needs are absolutely guaranteed by the most stringent of warranties, in the plainest, truest words: knock; seek; ask. But you must read the fine print. 'Not as the world giveth, give I unto you.' That's the catch."

—ANNIE DILLARD

Isaiah 29:13-16 (esp. 13)    John 16:23-24

If you had three wishes, what would you wish for? Do you remember this question from your childhood? Everyone would always say, "More wishes" or "infinite wishes" until the questioners grew wise and axed that option.

You'd toss out world peace so as not to appear selfish. Then you'd try to come up with something that engaged all your desires in two more wishes. Money was a big one, because enough of it would provide you plenty more wishes. But the game felt so flawed and limited. Why can't we have infinite wishes?

Jesus says, "You may ask me for anything in my name, and I will do it" (John 14:14 NIV).

Anything? What!? Jackpot! Jesus is a genie? We can present requests, whatever we want, and we get it. We don't even have that annoying caveat of "no additional requests." Then he stuffs Himself back into His lamp and leaves us to our own devices.

So what's this "in my name" piece? We don't want to have any qualifications popping up on us like the genie question. Genie Jesus appears too perfect, much like a Snickers with no fat or sugar.

Those three words might just change everything. Everything else Jesus says comes from another place; why wouldn't this also? As techno master Moby says, "No human being could ever come up with this." Jesus throws out lines like, "Pray for those who persecute you" (Matthew 5:44), "the world hates you" (John 15:19), and "turn the other" cheek (Matthew 5:39).

This Jesus might not be the genie I saw in *Aladdin*. He says crazy stuff that doesn't jive with what I want. His teachings aren't abolished when I want to do my own thing, and He doesn't cater to my every whim. He has His own agenda, and that agenda involved a cross.

So pray for some reconsideration. Prayer may not be about the pray-ers and their fantasies. It might mean aligning ourselves with Jesus in an "in my name" way. Maybe if we begin to understand Him, we might ask differently. We might ask for things that glorify Jesus' Father.

Go ahead and sell your lamp. He just won't stay in there. Jesus is neither a genie nor the a-volitional deity we'd imagined. He's real, wild, unpredictable, and He's taking us far beyond our petty wishes.

*Adam*

- Do *you* ask for things in *Jesus'* name? What does that mean, anyway?
- Why do *you* ask Him for anything?
- What might He want *you* to request? What might be His motives?

# DAY 43

# PROMISE OR POSSIBILITY

*"No man is an island, entire of itself; every man is a piece of the continent, a part of the main."*

—JOHN DONNE

| Matthew 18:18-20 | Ecclesiastes 4:9-12 |

Thomas Goodwin, the Puritan theologian and preacher, offered some simple advice regarding Jesus' promises: "Sue him for it."

If Jesus made a promise, we can act on it and tell Him, "You promised this."

Rarely will we because His promises involve living by His teachings (no small task), storing our treasure in heaven (what sort of returns will we get?), being blessed for various forms of poverty (OK, that's going too far), and agreeing with Him.

Jesus says if two or three of us agree on anything in prayer, it will be done (Matthew 18:19). That's an enormous promise. Perhaps that promise involves something as grand on our part.

Rarely do we think of faith as something communal. More rarely do we think of prayer as something communal, something we share and do together. Rather than think of ourselves as a body, we see ourselves as independent faith contractors, operating alone. Prayer is personal, private. But search the Scriptures. God hammers this idea of His people being together, teaching their children, following His steps. They read, listen, pray, fast, and feast together. Look at Jewish festivals; look at Jesus and the twelve in the upper room; look at the believers in Acts.

What's the power of two or three together? Put yourself in His place. You're the father. All the children agree on a common desire. When two children set aside their own agendas to present a joint petition, how can a father reject it?

We in the West sometimes see the world in conflict. We see Russians and Ukrainians, Israelis and Palestinians, Chinese and Tibetans, and Indians and Pakistanis at each other's throats. These macrocosms represent the individual, enacting great schisms. But agreement, the coming together of individuals, warms the Lord's heart.

Catholics and their cousins in faith, the Greek Orthodox, understand something of community. The group or body of faith is of paramount importance. The saving that God does involves a people, not just individuals.

That is no small task. That means setting aside our obsession with self and personal agenda. That means thinking together, with others. There's power in this unity.

Remember, He promised.

*Adam*

- To what extent do you pray with others?
- What fears, insecurities, pride, selfishness or dogma prevent you from doing so?
- Why does Jesus say that He is present in the midst of two or three people who gather in His name?

# DAY 44

# HEAR YOU, HEAR, YOU

"And I heard a voice saying, 'Come and see,' and I saw."

—JOHNNY CASH,
"THE MAN COMES AROUND"

| Mark 1:35 | Psalm 40:1-5 | Psalm 46:8-10 | Matthew 6:5-13 |

Two often people furiously clash over some words, meanings, or intentions, crossing paths of communication. It sounds like Capitol Hill during an election year. But they are closer than they think: classmates discussing a project, fraternity brothers checking expense accounts, or any man and woman fighting over semantics. Both parties desperately want the other to hear them, to receive their words and meaning.

Yet neither listen, choosing instead to speak and then shout more loudly. And with more volume. The volume is the problem. We can't hear. We won't listen. Maybe we don't want to because of our obsession with our agenda, our rights, our wants, and our selves. Maybe we've not learned how.

But just as we choose not to listen to others in a dispute, we are deaf to God. We present to Him our complaints, Christmas lists, and project assignments. We ask rhetorical questions, or in times of distress, accusatory.

Do we ever stop to listen to His response? Do we want a response, or do we look only for a result?

Prayer, talking with God, suffers because we don't listen. According to ancient documents, God spoke to people. He spoke to Adam, Noah, Abraham, Jacob, and Moses. He spoke to the prophets. What's more, these men listened more than they spoke. We have records of them talking to God, certainly, but the documents place greater emphasis on a speaking God than a listening people.

What's changed? Why do we not listen for God instead of talking at Him?

Who has time to listen? You don't dial God up and then hear His voice. This listening is more like waiting on Him to show up. That takes time, and we've got things to do. Doesn't He realize this is the twenty-first century, the modern and globalized world where time is money? There's not time to stop and listen for anything or anyone.

But God Himself speaks, and this is no small matter. He speaks to us, to you and me personally, individually. Is this not worth the time it takes to tilt our heads toward Him, away from our days and agendas? God speaks. Will we listen?

*Adam*

- **Do you look for God's response or simply results?**
- **Do you want to hear what God has to say?**
- **How do you listen?**

# DAY 45

# OREOS FOR BREAKFAST

"But if you try sometimes,
you just might find you get what you need."

—THE ROLLING STONES

| John 17 | Romans 8:26-27 | Hebrews 4:14-16 |

Moby, the singer-songwriter, once said that if given the choice as a child, he would've eaten Oreos for breakfast, ice cream for lunch, and Oreos mixed in ice cream for dinner. He would've been happy. Fortunately, his parents intervened.

Who doesn't relate to this in some way? We each want Oreos, ice cream, then Oreos and ice cream together, or something to that effect. We might call it a new car, or that particular someone we want to fall in love with us, or the right med school. From our vantage point, at 18, 26, 34, 49, 57 or 73, we usually know what we want and why it's best for us.

Fortunately, our Father remains engaged in raising His children.

Paul says the Spirit prays for us. The writer of Hebrews says Jesus prays for us, and in John, we see Jesus pray for the disciples and for future believers. This treads on deep mystery.

We don't really know God's will. (Do we even know ourselves?) We have a few ideas here and there, such as His desire for our love, that we love each other. Jesus, and then Paul, lay out how they want us to live. But in the daily grind, we feel like we're flying blind. Certain people cause us strange guilt when they tell us they know God's will, as if they have some Cliff's Notes version of it. You feel a little frustrated, uninvited to some party about the secrets of the universe, and you ask, "What's wrong with me?"

It will work out. You have desires, and sometimes those desires are for Oreos for breakfast. Sometimes you desire whole-wheat cereal with berries, flax seed, and goat's milk for breakfast. Either way, the Spirit continues to talk to the Father for you. He weaves together your crazy will with God's own will. And He takes a much longer view.

In the end, it all works together for your good, for my good (see Romans 8:28).

Remember, when we survey the landscape of our lives and ask questions, God remains engaged, intervening. Were He to leave us to our desires, we'd quickly find ourselves with blood sugar issues, rapidly approaching obesity and heart disease. We'd think He didn't care. Were He to simply impose His own will, we'd think He didn't care about our desires.

As it is, He cares about our hearts and our lives. He remains engaged.

*Adam*

- For what do you pray?
- How do you handle prayers that are not answered to your satisfaction?
- What do you imagine the Spirit prays for you?

DAY 46

# BALANCE

"What I dream of is an art of balance."

—HENRI MATISSE

| John 6:25-71 | Deuteronomy 8:3 | Acts 2:42-47 |

"Practice moderation in moderation," the yoga instructor repeated in a melodic chanting as she rhythmically struck the studio-sized miniature gong. My mom and I attempted to stay balanced as we stifled laughter. This exercise in relaxation stretched more than just our muscles and tightly wound tendons. Admittedly we were yoga novices, far more accustomed to a brisk run or lengthy bike ride.

Despite my inability to keep a straight face, I think back to those words that almost circumvent themselves. Moderation. Moderation in moderation because without moderate moderation, moderation fails to exist in the first place. It seems redundant, doesn't it?

Moderation in life equates to balance. And this balance is more than standing on one foot while reaching both arms above the head. This balance manifests itself in all areas. We are whole beings, and our continued existence requires necessary functions. We eat. We sleep. We work. We live in relationship with others.

Like spokes on a wheel, if any one of these areas extends too far, or is cut too short, the wheel ceases to be round. It can no longer roll with ease or roll at all. If we eat in excess, or starve ourselves, we damage the body. If we forgo sleep or sleep all the time, we transform into either a zombie or sluggard. We must live in careful balance to function well.

The spiritual life mirrors the physical life, or perhaps the physical life mirrors the spiritual life. Regardless, our intangible existence consists of a wheel with many spokes. Spiritual food and water consist of the Scriptures: reading, memorizing, studying, teaching, and meditating. We starve ourselves if we do not consume regularly.

Our spiritual sleep manifests itself in the rest found in fellowship with others. Translation: hanging out. Our souls find comfort and company in the presence of others. We figuratively let our hair down.

Exercise in our relationship with Jesus consists of being obedient, doing the things that God wants us to do. We learn the strenuous exercise of listening.

Finally, breathing shows itself as prayer. This aspect is most sublime. We fool ourselves into thinking we can survive without oxygen because we can hold our breath. But it does not work. It does not last. We faint.

All facets of spiritual growth are necessary, like their counterparts in the physical world. Pray that we have the awareness to meet our own needs. Otherwise, the wheel just won't roll.

*Adam*

---

- **What is prayer to you?**
- **How do you pursue these aspects of your spiritual life?**
- **Is any one component out of balance? Why?**

# THE WORK OF GOD

## DAY 47

# WAITING

"Hope begins in the dark, the stubborn hope that if you just show up and try to do the right thing, the dawn will come. You wait and watch and work: you don't give up."

—ANNE LAMOTT

| Exodus 24:12-18 | 1 Kings 19:1-18 | Romans 8:22-25 |

From traffic lights to lines in grocery stores, so much of life seems to consist of waiting. The minutes in between our daily activities consume a surprising chunk of our time. And this waiting frustrates us because we never scheduled it. I dread the day when everything takes so much longer than expected, and I complete only half of my to-do list. Waiting reminds us that it's not all about us. Another plan supersedes our own.

Whether we like it or not, we must wait on certain issues. Jesus tells us that it matters how we wait. He tells parables of the coming kingdom, of people who were caught unaware. He tells us to keep our lamps ready, because we must remain vigilant, in preparation for the unexpected. We must choose moment by moment, day by day, to stay awake for what the Lord is doing.

With practice, we can build our awareness of God through waiting. Instead of obsessing over circumstances out of our control, we can resolve to see the wait as a gift and be uniquely available to the Lord.

Waiting is not punishment. God uses waiting as an opportunity to refine our faith. Elijah waited forty days beside the mouth of a cave to hear God's still, small voice. Moses waited forty days on Mount Sinai before receiving the Ten Commandments. Waiting builds patience and humility in us: two things that don't come easily.

There will come a time when the waiting will be over, and the very plans of God will be made known. There will be no more confusion, frustration, or waiting. All will be revealed. The Apostle Paul writes: "Now we see but a poor reflection as in a mirror; then we shall see face to face. Now I know in part; then I shall know fully, even as I am fully known" (1 Corinthians 13:12 NIV).

In the meantime? Jesus told his disciples to live as though that time of revelation were upon us. He put it like this: "This is the work of God, that you believe in Him whom He has sent" (John 6:29). Believe that the plan works for your good, that the plan itself is good, and that the one who made it loves you.

*Amy*

---

- What things in your life do you feel you're waiting on?
- How are you waiting?
- What does is it look like for you to believe God in the midst of waiting?

# DAY 48

# BREAKING THE LAW

"Small men command the letter of the law.
Great men serve its spirit."

—J. C. MARINO

| Micah 6:8 | Matthew 23:23 | Romans 12:1-2 |

For a Judge, God sure had an interesting way of handling rules. God told Abraham to sacrifice his only son Isaac. He told Joseph to marry a pregnant woman. Jesus informed the Pharisees that He would tear down the temple.

Following His great resurrection, He told the disciples—most simply—to wait.

Jesus refused to judge the woman caught in adultery. He hung out with tax collectors, sinners, prostitutes and the like. He instructed them to pay their taxes to Caesar, of all people.

God has a history of challenging the religious convictions of the times. He crushes moral codes, along with the self-piety that deeply ingrains itself in the people who follow such codes. We expect Him to bring peace and propriety, still waters and green pastures. More often than not, He brings crisis.

At almost every turn, God says, "You think you know it all, but you have forgotten the most important things: kindness, justice, and righteousness—the things that are dear to Me."

How could God ask His anointed one, Abraham, to murder?

How could He ask His servant Joseph to marry a woman who was already with child?

God is God. And we should never forget it. He constantly elevates His people above their own powers, preoccupations, self-imposed limitations, and yes, their moral codes.

This is the difference between filthy rags and eternal riches. His will or ours? His unlimited powers or our meager ones? His values, codes and plans or our rigid and inflexible ones?

The question falls upon each one of us—Who is Lord of our lives? If our answer is God, are we willing to trust Him, His plans, His preoccupations, and His love? The answer is yes, by His grace.

*Brad*

---

- What human codes of conduct are you hanging on to that God is less concerned with?
- What beliefs hold you back from trusting His plans fully?
- To what extent do you believe that walking humbly, doing justice, and loving mercy are all it takes to live a fulfilled life?

# DAY 49

# OUR FAITH

"We do not create our destiny;
we participate in its unfolding."

—DAVID RICHO

| Isaiah 64:8 | Ephesians 2:8-10 | 2 Corinthians 12:9 |

"He could do no miracle there except that He laid His hands on a few sick people and healed them. And he was wondered at their unbelief" (Mark 6:5-6).

Where there was no faith, Jesus could not operate.

How can that be? Isn't He the Son of God? Are His works dependent upon our prayers, or better yet, dependent upon our faith? The question is not whether Jesus had sufficient power. As a member of the Trinity, He is completely God and completely human. The question is, did He choose to operate when there was no faith? It seems not.

If the work of God is truly to believe in the One He has sent (see John 6:29), then this puzzle all makes sense. We are the spectators (by faith), and God Himself is the player, the one who actually does something. Too often we think the reverse is true. We operate under a system that relegates God to the role of spectator while we make ourselves the player, the pray-er, the doer, and if all goes our way, the hero.

*Quatsch*, as the Germans would say. Nonsense.

He does the work. We simply pray and believe in Him. Then when the act is ripe for the picking, God prompts us to chime in on some trivial idea that will finalize the work He has set in motion from the beginning of time.

What a wonder that God would do the work and then pass the final act on to us, so we can ride on His coattails across the finish line and think ourselves winners. How utterly humbling for Him. Why does He do it? Maybe because He wants to see who we'll give the glory to. Will we bow and confess the truth, that God Almighty, Maker of the heavens and the earth, did the deed—using us as mere pawns? Or will we pat ourselves on the back, bask in the glory, and take credit for a work for which we are utterly incapable?

God is the potter. We are but lumps of clay. And how wonderful it is to feel His powerful but loving hands shaping us into His vessel.

*Brad*

---

- How has God asked you to collaborate on finishing some of His work?
- How much effort does it require?
- How have you noticed the hand of God guiding you through difficult times?

# DAY 50

# THE HEAVY LIFTING

"In addition to all this, take up the shield of faith,
with which you can extinguish
all the flaming arrows of the evil one."

—PAUL,

IN EPHESIANS 6:16

| Ephesians 6:10-18 | Hebrews 11:1-3 | Matthew 8:5-12 |

I sometimes ask young people revealing questions like "Who among you is the laziest? Who is the hardest working?" This one normally sets off a rousing debate.

Ponder the thought. When it comes to work, are you a lightweight or a heavy lifter? Having formerly employed lots of varying individuals, I would choose one hard-working heavy lifter over ten wimpy, complaining lightweights any day of the week.

If you're one of those lightweights, don't worry, you're in good company. Jesus, whose hiring practices were dreadful at best, chose a host of lemmings. He often referred to them as "Little Faiths." They constantly missed the point and often forgot about Jesus' power to perform the grandest miracles. Sometimes hours after the last miracle.

When Jesus chooses to bestow the Greatest Faith Award (the GFA), he picked a pagan Roman of all people (see Matthew 8). According to Jesus, faith is that invisible power that shows up when you least expect it, and from the person from whom you'd least expect it. But don't worry, the "Little Faiths" make a great comeback later in the story.

Jesus refers to faith as work. When asked how to do the works of God, Jesus says: "This is the work of God, that you believe in Him whom He has sent" (John 6:29). Aha. The heavy lifters are the Big Faiths in the work.

This shouldn't surprise us.

When Paul describes the outfit for spiritual war, he refers to the shield of faith. Paul chose from an assortment of words for shield to make his point. He chose *thureos*, a grand oblong shield carried by the heavily armed soldier. Consisting of two thick layers of wood, the thureos absorbed the flaming arrows and extinguished them. It was the ultimate protection of its day. But it was also heavy and cumbersome. The average infantryman would have to lug his shield over hill and dell for the next battle. This was no doubt tiring.

Faith often feels this way. It would be easier to roll over and give up. When everything beckons the other way, faith reminds us to believe, hold fast and take the narrow way. Ultimately, we find security in this faith.

"Believe in the one He has sent," Jesus exhorts.

Do the heavy lifting. The work is in believing.

*Brad*

- How is faith like heavy lifting?
- How does faith protect?
- How does holding up your faith make you tired sometimes? Describe one occasion.

# DAY 51

# WHAT A GOD WANTS

"If you promise never to leave,
you just might make me believe."

—SUGARLAND, "JUST MIGHT"

| Deuteronomy 30:15-20 | Jeremiah 7:21-28 | Jeremiah 11:1-13 | Hosea 14:1-9 |

One of our primary desires is our desire to be right. If others don't believe us, we'll try to prove them wrong. Few desires trump this need to prove what we believe to be true. We must have others believe us. And the closer they are to our heart, the more dire the need.

A friend worked with children at a church. He always wanted to help others, and he gave away much of his time to do so. After some involvement with the first-graders, he found out one child had accused him of inappropriate touching. Although the boy eventually admitted concocting the story for attention, my friend had to take a polygraph, speak with elders of the church, provide character references, and speak with police and attorneys. He couldn't brush aside the defeating frustration and mental paralysis he experienced as a result. Why would someone believe this about him? Why would someone think he had foul intentions? He knew the truth about himself and his actions. To prove it, he'd go to any length.

From the beginning, God said, "Believe Me. I care for you, and I want the best for you. Look around at all I've given out of My love for you: trees for shade, water for swimming, plants for tending, animals for farms and pets, and resources for transportation. Believe Me."

Like a man smitten, God sends these love letters to woo us who struggle to believe.

Since the beginning of time, God has struggled with unbelieving people who won't trust His truths. Certainly, it's been maddening, painful, and frustrating.

We've not walked with the Lord in the cool of the evening since we departed Eden. His question after the fall was, "Where are you?" He wanted us with Him. But we couldn't be with Him. Doubt about His love separated us, and fear kept us in hiding. It does even now.

Still, He says, "I'm here! And I love you and want you to talk with Me. I want this more than anything else. How do you want Me to prove it? I'll do anything. I'll come be with you. No, I'll become one of you. And if that's not enough, I'll die for you."

And He did it. He became a pauper baby, then a respected teacher and said, "The work of God is this: to believe in the one He has sent" (John 6:29).

Then we killed Him. Of course, He let us. Because He realized that if we killed Him, if He'd die for us, we just might believe He loves us.

We just might.

*Adam*

- What of Jesus' words don't you believe?
- Why don't you believe them?
- What about God loving you is hard for you to accept?

# DAY 52

# FOLLOW

"The important thing is this: To be able at any moment to sacrifice what we are for what we could become."

—CHARLES DUBOIS

| Luke 14:16-24 | Matthew 9:9 | Matthew 8:18-22 |

I deeply want to experience life. I want to fall in love, marry, have children, build a career, attend my kids' football games, eat dinner with them, send them to college, renew my vows with my wife, attend reunions, visit old friends, and sit on my porch on a large piece of land in the South with lemonade in my hand. I've painted pictures in my head, I want this so badly.

We all want something. The problem is our desires are too small. We want the visible, the things that prop us up in the minds of others, despite the greater reality of the invisible.

Jesus encountered this problem. He called men to follow Him, and they responded, "I've just gotten married. "Let me go be with my wife." "I've wanted this, and I finally have it. Let me enjoy this for a while." Men said to him, "I've finally attained financial freedom. Let me know it and bask in it." Other men said, "I need to honor the memory of my father. The duties of my family call to me." To which Jesus replied, "You are not worthy of My kingdom. Go your own way."

Yet when He called Matthew to follow Him, Matthew, too, was at work. Immediately, Matthew abandoned it all. He gave no two-weeks' notice, as far as we know. He didn't finish the assignments for the day or tell his boss where he was going. Who knows how many clients and accounts his company lost that day? Yes, the culture was worlds apart, but so was Matthew's willingness. James, John, and Simon responded similarly.

They were willing to leave behind what they were for what they could become. They were willing to let go of the present for a greater, albeit unknown, future. They were willing to exchange what was for what could come. They believed in what they could not see. Because they believed Jesus, their faith told them this was not risky but was the most reasonable course of action.

They gave up this world and all it had to offer for the unseen reality that Jesus promised. Jesus' disciples desired a better country, a new world (see Hebrews 11:15-16). They desired more and were willing to give up everything to pursue it.

Jesus offers not only the keys to the kingdom, but a home and citizenship there. He offers us a place that makes real our unfulfilled hopes for this world. But we must follow Him to that place we cannot see. He knows the way. His eyes can see. We are the blind ones.

My desire to fall in love, get married, and have children is a desire to know intimacy, and part of it is to know the purification that comes with such intimacy and experience. And these will prove beautiful experiences. But these are only shadows of the experience that comes from following Jesus in this world and into the next. They are shadows compared to the reality of walking with Jesus through those experiences.

I've always feared Jesus would return before I saw all of life unfold in this world. Perhaps I need to look a little more deeply at what I desire, and whom I desire. A better country awaits.

*Adam*

---

- What things would you not give up to follow Jesus? Why do you hang onto them so tightly?
- What do you think offers you more than Jesus can?
- How does not seeing Jesus' promises create challenges for you?

# DAY 53

# LIKING NEW

"When we become aware that we do not have to escape our pains, but that we can mobilize them into a common search for life, those very pains are transformed from expressions of despair into signs of hope."

—HENRI NOUWEN

| 1 Corinthians 13:11 | Isaiah 65:17 | 2 Corinthians 5:17 |

I called my former teacher to talk. My confession came quickly: "I don't think I've liked myself much over the years."

His reply startled me. "Son, I don't think many people like who they are. At least if they are being honest. That is why Jesus offers to make us new creatures."

*Is this true?* I wondered. So many others appear so composed, so at ease in their lives.

Then I thought about friends whom I love dearly but who don't always love themselves so much. The class president who is scared witless to ask a girl out. He feels shame at his trepidation. Or the friend who hasn't yet finished college in the decade since he graduated high school. He loathes his shortcomings. What of those wrestling addiction? They hate their dependence. The overweight guy makes everyone laugh at his jokes, so they won't laugh at him. Even the pretty girl who is a threat to all other girls. She feels alone.

Often we're ignorant of what we've done or endured.

"For I gave you an example that you also should do as I did to you," Jesus said (John 13:15). He loved, forgave, emancipated. He gave us these tools that transform us, tools to make us new. Witness His love for Zacchaeus in Luke 19, His emancipation of Peter from the guilt of his betrayal in John 21, or His forgiveness of the adulterous woman in John 8.

Do we forgive ourselves for failures in friendships? For wounding ourselves and others out of uncontrolled desire? For squandering money, time, talent, and opportunities? For circumstances and traits beyond our control? We treat ourselves and each other with contempt because of these failings and life fixtures.

Jesus says we've been forgiven, though we haven't begun to see ourselves as forgiven. We are burdened by our pasts, as people worth less. He offers us the chance to see ourselves differently, to see ourselves as He sees us, but we keep returning to the familiar grounds of guilt and self-loathing. Greed, lust, judgment, arrogance, jealousy, anger, selfishness, dissension, and ambition-worship occupy places in us. We don't like who we are as a result.

Will we follow Jesus into those places? Will we walk with Him into those parts of ourselves that won't change overnight, but require daily attendance, confession, forgiveness, transformation, and re-creation? If we're to love ourselves, and somehow others, we must do these things. We should enjoy the peace and joy from following Jesus' example. Self-help gurus all merit some respect, but Jesus alone will make us new, not just effective. Becoming new contrasts greatly with simply being re-worked and rearranged. As we become new, a freshness and health and an emergent cleanliness speak to the soul.

Lamentations 3:22-23 says God's mercies are new every morning. That's fortunate because so are our failures. If His mercies are new this morning, we can believe we're becoming new creations. We are people we can like, people whose lives respond to mercy and not guilt, to love and not the worries of the past.

*Adam*

---

- Do you like who you are? All of you?
- Who or what do you want to be?
- How does following the teachings of Jesus make you new?

## DAY 54

# TIME AND SAND

*"But to a man on a mountain road by night,
a glimpse of the next three feet of road may matter
more than a vision of the horizon."*

—C. S. LEWIS

| Deuteronomy 1:19-46 | Deuteronomy 2:1-7 |
|---|---|
| Psalm 27 (esp. 14) | John 11:1-46 |

Driving across the country, endless expanses of America pass by my window: farmland, deserts, lakes, pastures. A continuity establishes itself in the repetition of land: a mundane movie with no visible plot and scenery with no scene. As a kid with seatbelt strapped, I watched with steady disinterest, my mind calculating the remaining minutes before I could pose the question again: "Are we there yet?"

Some destination existed ahead, someplace known as Grandma's house or Colorado. Each exact location remained a mystery to me. I believed Chicago was a country. The rock quarry we drove over was undeniably the Grand Canyon. How disillusioning for me to discover that Arizona was thousands of miles from our drive along the Lake Michigan coastline.

In the Bible, God released the Israelites from slavery in Egypt. He took them to the desert with a destination called the promised land. Initial excitement over the newfound freedom quickly turned into doubtful grumbling over their delayed arrival. The Israelites measured time in miles of desert walked. They walked endlessly.

The scriptures don't say they walked for forty years, as though it was an immense distance but that they wandered because they were being taught a necessary lesson. Historians determined that the Israelites' journey could have been completed in two weeks. Two weeks.

Yet they wandered. They walked. If their arrival had come immediately, would they have recognized the extent of the promise?

Would they learn to trust God or fall back on idols again? Would they have held the capacity to truly savor the promise of the Promised Land? Could they have learned the desert lessons taught in discomfort while sitting comfortably in a familiar place?

We resist the deserts too. We choose comfort. We prefer to go to enviable destinations of our choosing when we gain a clear view of the end. When removed from an imperfect situation and placed in a season of uncertainty, we idealize the places we once lived instead of anticipating the arrival of something better. We wander in deserts of a less sandy nature. We walk along paths we would not have chosen, suspended in the waiting for fulfillment of a plan and a promise. We are called to wait, and we hate waiting. Frustration sets in. We are not where we were, but we are not where we want to be. We reside in that uncomfortable place called transition.

Did God forget us, or is His timing just different? What must we learn in this expanse of time and vista of sand? When will we understand that while the shortest distance between two points is a straight line, a curved, twisted, and winding path causes growth? Something awaits us in this desert. Something as elusive as a mirage but as real as the gritty sand under our feet. How good could this place perhaps be?

*Amy*

---

- What are the deserts in your life? The "imperfect familiar?" The Promised Land?
- Are you seeking meaning or are you grumbling over circumstance?
- What can you learn in these times?

# DAY 55

# THINGS OF GOD

"What have I become, my sweetest friend? Everyone I know goes away in the end. And you could have it all, my empire of dirt. I will let you down. I will make you hurt."

—TRENT REZNOR,
"HURT"

| 2 Corinthians 4:16-5:10 | Luke 16:10-15 | Matthew 19:27-30 |

What kind of employer is God? Compared to the world, He offers abysmal pay and benefits.

Working for the world pays. We receive insurance, stock options, pay raises, bonuses, and vacations. This in addition to steady income that can buy clothes, cars, and housing. Our names show up in print and in conversation. Professional and social cliques woo us. Our influence grows. The better we become at our work, the more we attain. The clothes turn designer, the cars' interiors leather, and the houses sit on larger lots.

God's work doesn't offer much of this. He promises to take care of us, sure, but He never mentions class A shares of

Berkshire Hathaway or nights at the Ritz. He doesn't always tell us what we're doing or where we're going. And there's not a lot of recognition or status involved. On the sliding social scale measuring attractive work, God's doesn't make the list. It's below unemployed.

God's work isn't about building financial empires but about building a kingdom. It's not focusing on projects and ventures but on finding purpose. It doesn't bring recognition, but it does mean recognizing Jesus in the world. Admission into the social elite doesn't come standard but feeling God's love does.

Power? No. Understanding personal weakness? Yes. It may not involve driving a Bentley, but it does mean walking with Jesus.

Man's work is visible, tangible, material, credible, and possible. Man's work is about producing things we can see. These things are the gods we make that tell us we're gods. They tell us we're alive, we exist, we matter, and our time here hasn't been wasted. They help us believe in ourselves. Then they die, and we need new gods.

God's work allows us to see the invisible, grasp the intangible, work for the immaterial, believe the incredible, and do the impossible. Ultimately, the work of God means believing in Jesus. This God doesn't die, He's checked that off His list already. And He alone can teach us how to really believe in ourselves.

See for yourself. Go work a lifetime building gods of security, comfort, and status. Watch them stand silent when you need them most. Watch history forget you and your influence.

There was a carpenter-teacher who lived two millennia ago. He lived among many exorbitantly wealthy men. No one remembers their names or their life's work. We still live in the shadow of His. Now, what does He say about work?

*Adam*

---◆---

- **What do you think valuable, lasting work is?**
- **Why are you working?**
- **How do you respond to Jesus' description of work in John 6:29? Why?**

# DAY 56

# INVISIBLE

"The cynic believes nothing at all."

—SOREN KIRKEGAARD

| 2 Corinthians 4:18 | Matthew 5-7 | Hebrews 11 |

Believing has never been the problem.
We believe in chairs. We sit in them. Ever had anyone pull a chair out from under you as you sit down? A "friend" did it to me once, in front of a roomful of people. How embarrassing. Yet I still believe a chair every time I sit on one.

We believe in cars. Reliable ones, anyway. We place our precious bodies into them, trusting that the brakes work. We simply don't weigh the potentially catastrophic consequences of brake failure.

And we eat food, fully believing that it won't harm us. Most processed American foods harm us in some way, but we don't worry.

What's so hard about believing? Why don't we always believe in our Maker? Why don't we believe that we turned out just as He intended? That our circumstances and the events in our lives are first sifted through the hands of a loving Father? That He has us just where He wants us?

The Apostle Paul gives us a few hints:

"For we fix our eyes not on what is seen, but what is unseen, since the seen is temporary, but the unseen is eternal" (2 Corinthians 4:18 NIV).

Or, "Faith is the assurance of things hoped for, the conviction of things not seen" (Hebrews 11:1).

Aha, it's those dadgum unseen things. We so badly want to believe in the unseen. But such faith eludes us. Not all of us are cynics when it comes to God. As Soren Kierkegaard pointed out, experience is a mixture of mistrust and love. Now and then we are inspired to believe the invisible, or to mistrust even the visible. Sometimes movies, books or stories help us out. We can envision going down Alice's rabbit hole or crawling through the wardrobe into C.S. Lewis's Chronicles of Narnia, or taking the red pill and finding our way out of the Matrix. Somehow these stories resonate with us. We know there is something more than what we see. Mankind has sought it out since the beginning of time. We have invented gods and religions to understand them.

While on Earth, Jesus spoke at length about the kingdom of heaven. He said that it was near (see Matthew 4:17); that it belongs to the poor in spirit (see Matthew 5:3) and to the persecuted (see Matthew 5:10); that those who practice the commandments will be great in the kingdom and those who don't will be called least (see Matthew 5:19); that you cannot enter the kingdom if your righteousness does not surpass that of the Pharisees and teachers of the law (see Matthew 5:20). And on and on and on.

Jesus wanted us to understand that His kingdom was the true reality, and that this world is a temporary shadow of that reality. He asks us to believe. Then believing becomes our work.

*Brad*

---

- What invisible things do you strive to believe?
- How do we increase our faith?
- Is God worthy of our trust? Why or why not?

## DAY 57

# BELIEF'S BABY

"The outer conditions of a person's life
will always be found to reflect their inner beliefs."

—JAMES LANE ALLEN

| Hebrews 11 | James 2:14-26 | Genesis 12:1-5 |
| Genesis 13:14-18 | Genesis 15:1-21 |

Belief produces. Though we cannot see, touch, or hear belief, we see the results it yields. Those results are the decisions and deeds that form our lives.

Look at Abraham. Called by a God he couldn't see to a land he'd never known, Abraham went. He left his family in search of a vague promise about blessings and curses. God didn't even tell him where He was leading him. He simply said, "Go to the land that I will show you."

Abraham found the land inhabited. Then God said, "It's for your offspring." But Abraham had no children. Still, Abraham believed. He trusted God's promise about a future child.

When Abraham walked through the deserts, God told him the land ahead would belong to his descendants. He believed this to be a good thing. He then heard God tell him he'd have a son—with his wife, Sarah. She had grown old with Abraham; she couldn't bear children. Of all the promises he'd heard, this sounded the most absurd. Sarah laughed.

When the son arrived, Abraham rejoiced. (Maybe more so because he saw a promise fulfilled.) Exultant, he named this son Isaac, meaning "laughter."

And then God seemingly reneged. He told Abraham to give back his son, to sacrifice him. He'd lived his entire life standing on promises, like a man stepping on stones to cross a river. Believing in their sturdiness, he proceeded, step by step. He stumbled at times in his humanity, but he believed for so long, he felt he could somehow obey once more.

God had brought Abraham this far, with Abraham living off the land and words from God: could he believe God with what was closest to his heart? With his killing knife set to plunge into his son's chest, Abraham heard God tell him to spare the boy. What God wanted, He said, was to see that Abraham wouldn't withhold his son from Him.

True belief, not mere assent, nudges us to decide and do. Will I really believe he'll provide if I take this job? When He says, "Wait," will I? Even though my life shatters? Will I speak when asked about my friendship with Jesus? Will I still love Him when sickness and pain and loss strike me? Or worse, one I love? Will I give what's closest to my heart if He asks for it?

These questions represent some of what our belief asks of us. But if we believe, belief yields results, and what we choose shows the depth of our belief. Belief leads our feet to the stones of Jesus' promises. We need to take one step after another. As God did with Abraham, He will guide each of us across our own river.

*Adam*

---·---

- What decision have you made based on belief in the last day, week, month, year?
- What decision have you made based on doubt or fear in that time?
- What is the one thing you don't believe? That He'll provide? That He knows where your road goes? That He's in control? That He loves your loved ones? That He'll give His Spirit?

# DAY 58

# DO YOU BELIEVE?

| Romans 10:1-13 | Mark 4:9-12 | Matthew 13:11-17 |

It's never a bad idea to take an inventory of what you believe. You might resonate with some of these ideas but not others.

Do you believe good grades make you a person who passes muster?

Do you believe your fraternity/sorority's letters make you special? Do you believe you're more cultured and civilized than that girl who comes from the boondocks?

Do you believe your job makes you more qualified to understand life and the world than the cashier at the grocery store?

Do you believe your involvement in campus ministry says you are more spiritual than those who aren't involved?

Do you believe leaving your hometown makes you wiser and more accomplished than your peers who remained?

Do you believe you have greater authority than others because you've traveled the world? Do you believe you're good enough—or too good—to date/marry anyone?

Do you believe your clothes tell people who you are? Not just something about you but all of you?

What about your car, your house, your job, your husband's job, or your wife's looks?

Do you believe your charity, your giving, proves you're a swell guy? Or does it make you a swell guy?

Do you believe you have it so much more together than others?

Why do you believe that extra fat on your tummy makes you less appealing to others?

Why do you believe happiness lives in New York, LA, DC, Chicago, Atlanta, or Seattle?

Why do you believe Ivy League grads have some intrinsic value I don't?

Why do you believe you need to work so hard to make people proud of you?

Why do you believe you need to win at everything?

Why do you believe you are better than those who drink? Do drugs? Sell drugs? Sell their bodies?

Why do you believe that corporate types and political bigwigs hold more value in the world than janitors and cafeteria workers?

Why do you believe you can know everything about someone from their actions?

Why do you believe the poor do it to themselves?

Why do you believe in capitalism so much? Do you believe you are a good person?

*Amy*

**DAY 59**

# LISTEN . . . CAREFULLY

"The strongest influences in my life are always whomever I love. Whomever I love and am with most of the time, or whomever I remember most vividly. I think that's true of everyone, don't you?"

—TENNESSEE WILLIAMS

| Genesis 3 | Matthew 4:1-11 | John 10:1-6 |

Eve heard the serpent speak. The problem wasn't the hearing. The problem lay in her choosing to listen. Thus, the serpent won the right to deceive her. Every person's story since entails a competition of voices. To what voice will we bend our ear?

The movie *A Beautiful Mind* depicts this struggle for a person's mind. John Nash is schizophrenic and spends years wrestling with the voices in his head and discerning truth from illusion. The voices never fully disappear; rather, Nash learns to ignore them.

Voices guide us through our lives. They tell us how to manage our social careers through the brutal halls of grade school, how to move ahead in the work world, how to provide for our appetites, and how to appease an upset conscience. They tell us to work harder, to achieve more, to make more money, to wear certain clothes, to treat enemies with contempt, to plan our lives, and to consider this life our own.

Jesus objects. Those voices are serpents in the garden. He tells us that we should believe, give to the poor, stop worrying about what we will wear, cease obsessing over appearance, love our enemies, deny ourself, and take up our cross. Listen to His voice, for it is the one that gives life.

We make choices every day. To whom will we listen: *Cosmo, Maxim,* MTV, *Fortune,* and Madison Avenue? Do they want what's best for us or just our money? Because we hear them everywhere.

Jesus calls us to deny these voices. He asks us to watch for truth and love, even when it comes from the vitriol-spewing atheist. He also warns us to watch for deception, even when it comes from the preachers and teachers of God's Word.

He seeks shrewd and ever-present vigilance. He asks a lot. But in return, He tells us we'll find truth, we'll find life, we'll find the way.

*Adam*

---

- **To whom do you listen and why?**
- **How have those voices shaped your identity and purpose?**
- **Who do you believe speaks from a place of truth and love? How do you know?**

## DAY 60

# EMMAUS

> "God is in the slums, in the cardboard boxes
> where the poor play house. God is in the silence
> of a mother who has infected her child with a virus that
> will end both their lives. God is in the cries heard under
> the rubble of war. God is in the debris
> of wasted opportunity and lives."
>
> —BONO

Matthew 18:18-20 | Luke 24:13-35 | Matthew 28:16-20

Everything changes. That's the result of believing Jesus. When we begin to see life through the lens of Jesus' teachings, people change. Incorrigible scoundrels look less like lost causes and more like neglected children. Those who seemed powerful and wealthy often appear poorer and somewhat pathetic. The dealers in drugs and guns seem more scared, more hurt. Through the lens of Jesus, you can see Jenna Jameson's plea: "All I've ever wanted is for people to love me."

What thrills when you look through the lens of Jesus is Jesus. He is everywhere.

Kanye West may have glimpsed this: "to the hustlas, killers, drug dealers, murderers, even the strippers… Jesus walks with them."

Jesus walks among us, and for some reason, He hasn't much interest in being exclusive or belonging to members-only clubs. He has not forgotten the cheats or stained lobbyists. He sees and walks with gun runners, warlords, child soldiers and child prostitutes. Such have always been those He has sought out—the broken, the failed, the rejected, and the morally unacceptable. Maybe they're more ready to receive Him than those who "have it together".

He loves people of all nationalities, backgrounds, and walks of life. And though we claim to own the rights to Jesus, He's free to like people of all religions.

You'll begin to see Jesus in situations you thought needed Him most. The places you desperately want him to go, He's already there. Compton and Las Vegas. The LA riots of '91. Bourbon Street. The red-light district of Amsterdam. Back alleys and bordellos. He frequented such locales two thousand years ago; He's still there.

It will take time to grow accustomed to seeing Jesus in these places we thought too dirty, too sick, or too sinful for Him.

It will take longer to believe that He identifies Himself with the people in these places. He said, "whatever you did for one of the least of these brothers and sisters of mine, you did for me" (Matthew 25:40 NIV).

*Adam*

- Where is the last place you expect to find Jesus? Why?
- How does seeing Jesus in such a place change the way you treat others?
- When have you encountered Jesus in "one of the least of these"?

**DAY 61**

# THE BEGINNING AND END OF WORK

*"Work isn't to make money; you work to justify life."*

—MARC CHAGALL

| Genesis 2:15-17 | Genesis 3:13-24 | John 6:25-40 (esp. 28-29) |

Two people chose not to believe. Life has been toilsome since. But not just in the physical and material realm. The fall incurred the curse of work. The earth resists us, and we labor for enough food to eat today. Tomorrow, we begin it again. No day arrives when we say, "I have done enough. My work is finished." We always need more.

Man's curse is to struggle in his work. Women's curse involves another kind of work: pain in childbirth and a male dominated world. Today, many women seek freedom in competition with those men in multiple arenas. The curse continues.

Since the dawning of time, we've worked. Doing so remains necessary. Yet Jesus unveiled the true nature of God's work. He told us that belief is God's great task for humanity. Because God has said He loves us, and that He meets our needs, we alone are not responsible for them. Believing this involves work from the very outset.

God told Adam and Eve that if they didn't listen to Him, they'd perish. They did, and we do. We die a little every day when we believe the lie that we alone care for ourselves. The struggle and isolation steal our life; we need God's words as daily sustenance because we need His friendship, His nurturing care.

Jesus wants His children to believe that God cares, speaks, and listens (see John 9:31). You've worked far too long, mistakenly believing you're alone. Come back to your original purpose and walk with God once more. Know that He loves you and is there for you.

A curse exists. It separates us from our maker. Oftentimes, we feel we know little else than this curse. Yet on a hill called Calvary, Jesus became a curse for us that we might walk away from ours. The curse still tells us that we'll work through sweat to eat bread from the ground. We'll then die. Jesus tells us that He is the bread we really need (see John 6:35). When we seek nourishment in Him and His presence, we'll begin to live. We'll leave behind the fears that drive us to care for ourselves all our days.

He tells us to believe in Him, to believe this. No wonder He calls it the work of God.

*Adam*

- What is your idea of God's work?
- Have you come to a place of believing that feels like labor? Explain.
- What does believing look like from Jesus' point of view?

# DAY 63

# TEACHERS

> "You're afraid of me. You're afraid I won't love you back. You know what? I'm afraid too. . . . I want to give it a shot. At least I'm honest with you."
>
> —SKYLAR IN GOOD WILL HUNTING

John 1:35-39 | 2 Kings 2:1-12 | John 8:31-47 (esp. 31-32)

We don't remember what we learned in school. We remember the hard lessons of the hallway or the cafeteria lunch table. But little of the chalkboard and exams remain with us. That only lingers when the teacher engages us where we live.

In the movie *Good Will Hunting* gifted Will has two teachers. Professor Lambeau wants to facilitate Will's prodigious mind. Community college sage Sean hopes to help Will's humanity. He seeks to teach something of healing and hope. Will is a genius. And he's broken. Abused and abandoned repeatedly as a child, he now abuses and abandons others.

One teacher cares about Will's ability. The other cares about his soul. Sean, the teacher who's experienced real pain, possesses the tools to lead Will out of his isolation and fear. Will doesn't become a Nobel Laureate as Lambeau hopes. Over time, he does begin to become free and alive.

Sean enters the place where Will lives, where he hurts. Sean leads him out, because he has walked the same path, been through the same pain, and he survived with awareness.

We all have some of Will in us. We will admit there's something broken in us, and most also admit we can't repair it. We need the Seans to expose our inner world, the place where we live, and help with the healing. Most of us, however, find only Lambeaus who, while well intentioned, only help us with our abilities, leaving us in our brokenness.

Jesus has known brokenness. He's also known love and wisdom and joy. He taught these qualities to a few broken people some years ago, and it changed their world. It changed ours too.

Might Jesus still have something to teach us about life? Can He still take us over the terrain He's traversed? The difficulty for us, as for Will, lies in believing this Teacher is worth the risk.

He asks us to open our closed fists to embrace an abusive world. He tells us we need to move through pain not away from it. He instructs us to give if we want to receive and to die if we want to live. That's crazy. That's risky. And we know from the past that the stakes are high, but the benefits are real.

*Adam*

- Who has taught you the most about life?
- Who or what has required you to take the greatest risks?
- What from Jesus' teachings strikes you as risky?

# DAY 64

# DO I REALLY BELIEVE?

"I'm finding more and more truth in the words written in red. They tell me there's more to life than just what I can see. Oh, I believe."

—BROOKS AND DUNN, "BELIEVE"

| Zephaniah 3:17-20 | Isaiah 49:14-16 | 1 John 3:1-3 |

Do I really believe...
     That Jesus abides in me? That I abide in Him?
That He cares more about love and mercy than service and sacrifice?
That He believes in me? That he believes I can be like Him? And calls me to be like Him?
That God's Spirit leads me, guides me, comforts me?
That He considers me a friend?
That the world will know I follow Him if I love others?
That people will persecute me for following Him?
That in Him I have peace?
That believers can truly become one?

That He is present with me in my pain?
That I have overcome the world?
That God's love is perfected in me when I love others?
That He has conquered death?
That He's worth leaving everything behind to follow?
That He knows my heart and thoughts? And still loves me?
That He wants me to love my enemies?
That receiving a child in His name is receiving Him?
That clothing the naked, feeding the hungry, visiting the sick or imprisoned is doing so to Jesus?
That He gives me what I need?
That much is required of them to whom much has been given?
That I need to repent?
That He wants me to love Him more than anything else in my world?
That He'd leave 99 to find me?
That I can't serve both God and money?
And that He's enough?

*Adam*

**DAY 65**

# REMEMBER NOT TO FORGET

"The world will little note, nor long remember what we say here, but it can never forget what they did here. It is for us the living, rather, to be dedicated here to the unfinished work which they who fought here have, thus far, so nobly advanced."

—ABRAHAM LINCOLN,
GETTYSBURG ADDRESS

| Deuteronomy 6:1-9 | 1 Samuel 7:1-13 | Matthew 26:26-30 |

God blesses and provides. People forget.

What is it that causes us to forget the fundamental experiences of our life?

Scientists say that forgetting is essential to the human mind. As the brain filters literally millions of experiences each year, it must offload less essential information. The brain filters out trite and painful info-bits, not unlike a computer, in an attempt to keep the "hard drive" clean.

Orthodox Jewish people post a decorative box containing important Scripture verses on their doorframes and gates. They tie leather boxes containing important Scripture verses on their foreheads. In ancient times, they built stone piles to remember their victory over the Philistines. Jesus asked His apostles to eat bread and drink wine in remembrance of Him.

As we age, we realize how much work it takes to remember. We must write things down and ask for reminders. And the influx of information continues. We attempt to sip small amounts of information from gushes of the proverbial fire hydrant.

Years ago, our family was spared. Our second son, Ben, fractured a vertebra while jumping on a friend's trampoline. For his efforts, he was rewarded with a helicopter ride to Baltimore's shock and trauma unit. Despite three fractures, the bone remained stable, and he experienced no neurological damage. We are exceedingly grateful. In the first couple of weeks, we said a little thank-you prayer every fifteen minutes. After a couple months, we gave thanks about once a week. Today, we exhale a sobering sigh periodically. In a couple years, it'll be just another blip on the radar. In a couple decades, it will barely register.

That's why the visuals are essential. We need photos. We should reread journals regularly. God taught Israel to create holidays that require them to recall.

And when we do look back, we realize that life is a series of waves. There are crests and troughs. But our understanding of the waves is counterintuitive. As time goes on, we realize that the troughs are actually crests. The best times are when crests are disguised as troughs. When life hangs in the balance is when we grow the most. And such revelations are most often grasped in hindsight.

There's one thing we should remember about these times: don't forget.

*Brad*

---

- Describe some formative experiences in your life.
- Do you recall them regularly? How have they impacted your life?
- How can you remember them better?

# THE KINGDOM OF GOD

# DAY 66

# THE KINGDOM

"I asked the heavens, the sun, the moon, and the stars: "We are not the God whom you seek," said they. To the things that stand around the doors of my flesh I said, "Tell me of my God! Although you are not He, tell me something of Him!" With a mighty voice they cried out, "He made us!" My question was the gaze I turned on them; their answer was their beauty."

—AUGUSTINE'S CONFESSIONS
(BOOK 10, CHAPTER 6)

| Matthew 13:31-34 | Matthew 5:1-12 | Matthew 6:28-34 |

What is the kingdom that Jesus talks about? Where is it located? How long does it take to get there? What is the official language? The currency? The colors of the flag and the tune of the national anthem? When Jesus refers to this place, we think of a tangible location, yet His descriptions provide little in terms of clarity and description.

It's a paradox really. In His Sermon on the Mount, Jesus claims, "Blessed are the poor in spirit for theirs is the kingdom of heaven." Poor in spirit? These people inherit the kingdom? In my world the strong rule and the proud conquer. They take by force and maintain power in the same way.

Throughout the book of Matthew, Jesus offers pictures to describe the kingdom. Perhaps these illustrations, while providing nothing in the way of a complete description, offer the most accurate portrayal. In pictures and through metaphor, the truth emerges, shining out of the multi-faceted descriptions and allowing for depth and interpretation. "The kingdom of heaven is like a mustard seed" (13:31) and "like yeast" (13:33).

If I wanted to attract tourists to my kingdom, my pitch would vary greatly from these descriptions of small, unassuming items. While seemingly tiny and insignificant, upon examination, both a mustard seed and yeast pack potential. Mustard seeds grow into prolific plants. And yeast, when added to dough and left to rise, expands exponentially. It is alive and brings growth.

I once heard someone say, "If we could see what was on the other side, we would give all of this up in a second." Perhaps that is what the kingdom is, the vision to see the invisible, the trust to believe that in weakness there is strength, in poverty of the spirit there is inheritance. What does it take to live in this reality? To believe that if I seek first the kingdom that everything else ensues? I think about the black-and-white optical illusion drawing. Some people see two faces. Other people see a vase. And both are right depending on the focus. The black parts show two faces while the white space in between reveals the outline of a vase. Focus. Perspective. The vision to look beyond…

*Amy*

- How can we see the kingdom?
- How do we live in the kingdom while on earth?
- What are the characteristics of the kingdom?

# THE HOLY SPIRIT

# DAY 67

# THE GREATEST ADVENTURE

"To fall in love with God is the greatest romance; to seek him the greatest adventure; to find him, the greatest human achievement."

—ST. AUGUSTINE

| 2 Timothy 2:11-13 | Ephesians 2:1-5 | 2 Corinthians 4:11 |

God loves adventures.

Who of us cannot relate to Frodo, and his best-friend sidekick Samwise Gamgee? Frodo, the impulsive hero on a mission to deliver the Ring of Power, and Samwise Gamgee, who recognizes that he cannot be the carrier of the ring, but he can carry his friend Frodo. Chapter after chapter in Tolkien's *Lord of the Rings* trilogy, the steady Samwise keeps his friend Frodo on the rails, despite his frequent diversions.

Or who cannot relate to the four children who visit Narnia through the wardrobe in C. S. Lewis' *Chronicles of Narnia*? They meet Mr. Tumnus, a gracious faun, who leads them to other friendly creatures, including Mr. and Mrs. Beaver. He also warns them of the White Witch, and her vast skullduggery.

Somehow these adventures draw us in, but we forget that we are on an adventure of our own. Every day we meet Mr. and Mrs. Beaver in dozens of forms. We witness the wily deeds of the White Witch. When we see life in this frame, it rescues us from the day in, day out boredom that comes from our general sleepwalking through the motions.

Wouldn't it be better if we maintained a posture of readiness? What if we were constantly looking about, consulting our Samwise sidekicks, and figuring out why Aslan has connected us to Mr. and Mrs. Beaver again?

We hope for lives of bravery and courage, but bottom line, we are just dumb, helpless, defenseless sheep. When our bodies exhibit bravery and courage, it is because our hearts have been filled up with Jesus Himself. His bravery and courage pulse in our veins. If we allow Him, He will live out His life through us.

A hero of mine, Dr. Richard Halverson, described his morning routine once. When he rose in the morning, he went to his study and read the Scriptures, then he prayed, attempting to give every small portion of his being to God for that day. One at a time, he consciously offered God his body, his mind, his energy, his money, his possessions, until he had nothing else to give. He literally dumped all that he was and all that he had on the table in front of God. Then he would ask God to clothe him with Jesus, so that Jesus could live out His life through Richard.

Paul writes to Timothy that "If we have died with Him, we will also live with Him" (2 Timothy 2:11). When we understand this, we have all that it takes to live a life of great adventure.

*Brad*

---

- What does a posture of readiness look like to you?
- What themes can you identify in your journey?
- **In what way might you be fixated on the next page, instead of the current one?**

# DAY 68

# THE ULTIMATE MULTI-TASKER

*"You cut me down to size and opened up my eyes, made me realize what I could not see."*

—COLDPLAY,
"SWALLOWED IN THE SEA"

| Romans 8 | 1 Corinthians 2:9-16 | John 16:7-16 |

A great juggler invokes the awe of the audience. Multiple balls fly through the air in various patterns. Bowling pins and blazing batons are thrown and caught and maneuvered with improbable flawlessness and skill. The crowd watches in wonder. How can he keep so many balls in the air? How come he never drops the bowling pins? Why doesn't he feel the heat of the blazing batons?

The Holy Spirit juggles much the same way, according to the Scriptures. No one has more balls in the air. He:

- Counsels (John 14:26).
- Teaches us and reminds us of everything Jesus said (John 14:26).
- Convicts the world of guilt (John 16:8).
- Guides us into truth (John 16:13).
- Speaks only what He hears and tells us what is yet to come (John 16:13).
- Takes from what is Jesus' and makes it known to us (John 16:14).
- Searches all things, even the deep things of God (1 Cor. 2:10).
- Helps us understand what God has freely given us (1 Cor. 2:12).
- Lives in us, His temples (1 Cor. 3:16).
- Fills us (Eph. 5:18).
- Is a deposit from God, guaranteeing what is to come (2 Cor. 5:5).
- Leads us, making us sons of God (Romans 8:14).
- Testifies with our spirit that we are God's children (Rom. 8:16).
- Helps us in our weakness and intercedes for us (Rom. 8:26).
- Testifies about Jesus (John 15:26).
- Circumcises the heart (Rom. 2:29).
- Is the seal of our inheritance (Eph. 1:13-14).
- And much, much more.

That's a fair bit. Not to mention that the Spirit is multi-faceted yet specific, working in my life personally, deeply, insightfully, patiently, uniquely. And He does the same in yours.

A power resides in our hearts about which we, admittedly, know very little. In the hustle and bustle of twenty-first-century America, we easily ignore the Spirit. He works softly, aided by solitude. His presence increases as we seek to understand Him. Those who heed Him are caught up in the wonder and delight of this amazing person.

*Brad*

---

- **Does the Holy Spirit live in you?**
- **If so, how do you experience His presence?**
- **What is He doing in your life today?**

# DAY 69

# SEALED

"Fear makes strangers of people who would be friends."

—SHIRLEY MACLAINE

| Ephesians 1:15-23 | Isaiah 61:1-3 | Acts 2:38-39 |

Perhaps our fears, when we peel them down to their core, come from forgetting. We fear that we'll be forgotten by those who care for us or should care for us. The greatest fear is that God will, or has, forgotten us.

For the moment, we can look around and say, "I think He is here. He hasn't forgotten me today. For now, I can trust Him, experience His presence."

But we don't think we can trust Him with the future.

We think, *He won't be there when I get there, to that place just beyond tomorrow. He'll forget, He'll leave, He won't know what He's doing, or He won't care anymore. The world is falling apart with war, corruption, poverty, disease, politics, and pain in general. God won't always have it in hand. He'll drop me, or He'll allow this to fall on me.*

But God gave us a promise, knowing that we fear tomorrow, and life, and whether He will wait for us, just over the hill. He didn't promise we'd live free of war, corruption, poverty, disease, bureaucracy, or pain. In fact, the gospels indicate that these things will, and must, come. Yet we have a promise. God gave us a pledge that in the face of all of this, He'd hold onto us. He won't forget; He won't leave; and He won't be overwhelmed. He promised that in the end, we'd be all right. We'd be with Him.

To prove this, He gives a pledge. Think of it as the most valuable collateral anyone could offer. He gave a piece of Himself. He gave His Spirit. The gift of the Spirit says to us, "You're loved. You're not abandoned. Better days await, and I will stay with you."

As fears mount, engage them. With His promise in hand, His contractual obligation before you, what is there to fear?

Collin Raye's song "Love Me" comes to mind.

He won't let us down. And He's loving us still. He's promised.

*Adam*

---

- Do you fear God won't come through?
- Or do you trust Him enough to make good on His promises?
- Does God's collateral convince you of His agreement to meet you after tomorrow? Why or why not?

**DAY 70**

# ARE YOU FULL?

"Sin is not hurtful because it is forbidden,
but it is forbidden because it is hurtful."

—BENJAMIN FRANKLIN

| 1 Corinthians 3:10-17 | Ephesians 5:15-20 | Ezekiel 36:24-32 |
|---|---|---|
| (esp. 16) | (esp. 18) | (esp. 27) |

At some point in our childhood, we hear a story about a bird. Why we hear this story, anyone can guess. Perhaps one generation feels the need to illustrate problem-solving for the next. The bird (a raven or a crow) grows thirsty. To his delight, he discovers a jar of water. To his dismay, the jar is half full. His beak is too short to reach the water, and he can't lift the jar to his mouth. Ever a shrewd animal, according to the fable-tellers, the crow or raven begins to drop rocks into the jar. With each rock, the water level rises. The stones displace the water and move it up to the thirsty bird's mouth because contrary states cannot coexist. Where the rock is, the water cannot be.

In the same way, sin cannot coexist with the Spirit. Sin overcomes the Spirit in us. The apostle Paul told his friends in Ephesus not to get drunk with wine. He told them to fill themselves with God's Spirit. This same Paul told his friends in Corinth that people who love and follow God become God's temple, His house. As such, God's Spirit lives in people as His home. If the Spirit resides in the temple, no room remains for sin. If we fill our lives with sin, we diminish the Spirit, push Him out of His own house, no less.

God created us to run on His Spirit. He designed us with His Spirit in mind. If we insist on denying the Spirit in our lives, choosing instead badness, let us not be shocked when we feel no great love, no throttling energy, no lasting pleasure, and no real zip in our lives.

Don't seek any quick answers here. How you fill your life with the Spirit, like any other matter of relating to people, involves all the nuances and uniqueness of a relationship. But we can understand how to begin. Create space in yourself, in your life. Move out the bad stuff and make room for the Spirit in you.

*Adam*

---

- What is the character of things that fill your life? What is their nature?
- How do the Scriptures explain the nature of someone filled with the Spirit (Galatians 5)?
- What is the result of someone filled with badness or sin? Someone filled with the Spirit?

# DAY 71

# KUDZU

"What we call failure is not the falling down,
but the staying down."

—MARY PICKFORD

| Revelation 3:11-22 (esp. 19-20) | Titus 3:3-8 (esp. 5) | Romans 12 |

You will not reach perfection in this lifetime. How much heartache could we avoid if we would teach this?

Have you ever seen kudzu? Congress thought it would be great to combat soil erosion because it grows anywhere and quickly. It now covers the South. Some people sow frustration by planting spiritual kudzu. People who tell us perfection sits within reach are planting invasive seeds. They tell us it's attainable. They say we can live without blemish, reach a state free from ugly desire, and slough off the cravings of our eyes. This, we think, will lead us away from failure and mistakes. We can do everything God wants, everything He says we should.

People water this kudzu each time they scorn someone's stumbling. They fertilize it when they hold up a fictional ideal of an unblemished life. Kudzu frustrates and brings despair; you continually must cut it back. Falsehood does the same to us.

Eventually, having heard enough of this talk from others, we learn to care for the vine ourselves. We chastise ourselves for every slip, every fall. And that rogue vine starts suffocating everything under it. We think, *Something is wrong with me. God doesn't like me, because I am not like the perfect people.* Self-hatred finds root and grows.

Kill the vine at its roots. Know that you will not reach perfection here. We will fall. We will turn away from God's teaching. But we can grow.

If this sounds too much like Rasputin's sin-so-grace-may-abound philosophy, it's not. The impossibility of attaining perfection or walking without stumbling does not license us to do whatever the mood desires. It does, however, free us from the burden of seeking perfection. After we stop wrestling with the constantly creeping vine of perfectionism, we confront another kind of kudzu. When we slip or fall, we'll hear a voice saying, "Just stay down. You're going to do it again, so you might as well quit fighting it. Save yourself the striving." We hear it each time we stumble.

For how many people does this failure authorize what they believe is wrong? "I've done it before, so I might as well again." "I blew it, I lost it, I'm not perfect. Why go back?"

Keep cutting the vine back. Continue resisting the clarion call to lie down, to give in. Keep going back to the God we wound. He keeps waiting, like a father watching his infant learn to walk. Stumbles and falls will come. But each new ascent matures us.

You will stumble. Growth may even require it.

*Adam*

---

- How does perfectionism suffocate someone? How has it suffocated you?
- Why is returning to God, getting up after we fall, so difficult?

**DAY 72**

# SENSITIVITY

"The finest qualities of our nature, like the bloom on fruits, can be preserved by only the most delicate handling. Yet we do not treat ourselves nor one another thus tenderly."

—HENRY DAVID THOREAU

| 1 Thessalonians 5:16-24 (esp. 19) | Acts 7:48-53 (esp. 51) | Ephesians 4:25-32 (esp. 30) |

When I was single, I viewed marriage differently than my hitched friends. The conditions of this institution left me baffled. Perhaps the seemingly complex and intricate interactions of two persons should not shock me so much, but they did.

What dizzies me? The little things that set two people spinning. Someone says something without thinking. The resulting frustrations amplify themselves beyond normal proportion. I feel like when I was a child, and I could never see the pop-up T-Rex in those squares of orange and yellow that looked like squares of orange and yellow. "I just don't see it," I used to say. "Magical Eye" was never magical to me.

But married people move exceptionally close to one another. The nakedness of bodies symbolizes the nakedness of the souls. Serious self-revelation occurs. Each asks in the giving, "You won't hurt me, will you? You're going to care about me and not push me away, right?"

This unclothing of the heart leaves it much more susceptible to scrapes and bruises. Thus, "The meatloaf is undercooked," or "You didn't feed the dog," come off as personal rejections. Somewhere between the spoken and the assumed, someone hears, "You don't love me."

When God gives His Spirit as collateral, we have an obligation to treat Him with tenderness, with sensitivity. God approaches unguarded when He gives this part of Himself.

"Don't hurt me, for I have come to be near you. I am jealous, but I won't force you. Please don't walk away. I care about you intensely, and this caring can help you live with such caring, such intensity. Don't crush this."

If this sounds like something you've witnessed before, that makes sense. Rejected lovers cry out in pain, call aloud for reinstatement of intimacy. God does not hurt us because He is like us; we experience pain because we are like Him.

He's approaching each of us. He comes honestly and vulnerably and naked of heart.

"You won't hurt me, will you? Will you care and not push me away?"

He knows we will. Still, he approaches.

*Adam*

- What grieves God's Spirit?
- How do you resist Him? Why?
- How can you fan the Spirit's flame in your life?

**DAY 73**

# CHOCOLATE OR VANILLA?

*"Liberty, taking the word in its concrete sense, consists in the ability to choose."*

—SIMONE WEIL

| Isaiah 30:21 | John 16:5-16 | Romans 8:1-27 |

"You have two options," he said, "chocolate or vanilla ice cream. Which do you choose?"

"Chocolate," she replied.

He asked why, and she gave her reason.

He repeated his initial question: chocolate or vanilla? Her answer came with a different reason. They repeated this back and forth twenty or so times. Finally, having asked "Chocolate or vanilla?" and hearing the response "chocolate" once more, he again asked why.

"Because I choose chocolate! That's why."

"Good. You've just made the first choice of your life."

Choosing is difficult. We usually don't choose anything, we just eliminate the other options and go with what's left. We place a matrix of criteria over our options and pick what aligns most closely. That way, when things go sour, we look back at the choice and say, "Well, it seemed like the best option at the time." We don't invest in our answer, so over time, we have no ownership of it.

These choices show up every day. Choices about where to go to school, what fraternity to pledge, what job to take, whom to date, whom to marry, where to live, or what to eat for dinner. We cannot say, "I choose this path, this person, this behavior."

Whether because of our selfishness or neurotic attempts to select the very best available, we stop at the precipice of choosing. Such decisions don't constitute a life of purpose.

The Spirit enables us to choose. The Spirit helps us see through the haze of life's options and know which way to go. The Helper, as Jesus called Him (see John 14, 15, and 16), makes options distinct. A paradox exists in God's business dealings: we gain some sort of ownership in our life when we give ownership to Him.

What does this yield? If we listen closely, and if we'll obey, we can act with some measure of boldness, of decisiveness. We can make distinctions and act on them as we walk with this guiding Spirit. We can discern truth and the good.

Finally, once we choose, we begin living authentically, because we have started our true volition. Option elimination doesn't determine action. We enter a different kind of adulthood where we assume some ownership over our lives. These are the first steps. And these only come when we listen for and follow the Spirit's guiding.

So what'll it be: chocolate or vanilla?

*Adam*

- How do you choose?
- Do you feel peace with your choices? Why or why not?
- When do you ever feel (and respond to) a leading regarding a choice?

# OTHER TOPICS

# DAY 74

# THE WEDDING AT CANA

*"Random acts of kindness in fact
reflect the heart of God."*

—ANONYMOUS

| John 2:1-11 | John 3:30 | Proverbs 11:24-25 |

Two things strike me when I read about the miracle of Jesus turning the water into wine. The physical transformation stands out, for sure, but it's the circumstances sparking the miracle that catch my attention. The wedding event says something specific about Jesus as a person.

I don't claim to be an expert on the ancient Near East, nor on Jewish culture and customs, but I have difficulty understanding why Jesus' mother thought He should involve Himself. Any host would feel embarrassed to run out of provisions for his guests, but does this really qualify as a moment for divine intervention? Doesn't the Lord have more important things on His agenda than an open bar?

Yet Mary thought this merited the attention of her Son. She said, "They have no wine." She didn't say anything else, but from Jesus' response, we can tell she implied more.

"They have a problem, and they need help. The bridegroom certainly does, given that some of his reputation rests on how well he can entertain. Won't you help them?"

Mary had a precious sensitivity. Jesus did as well and saw fit to bless the people at the wedding in general, and the bridegroom in particular. The opportunity He chose, providing more wine, wasn't one of life or death. But it communicated affection.

Jesus provided somewhere between 120 and 180 gallons of the finest wine, depending on the size of the waterpots. Yet who received the credit for this wine? The bridegroom.

"The headwaiter called the groom, and said to him, 'Every man serves the good wine first, and when the people have drunk freely, then he serves the poorer wine; but you have kept the good wine until now' " (John 2:9-10).

Honor fell on this man. Jesus chose to receive no credit for the gift of the wine. He didn't ask for any sort of gratitude. He gave even that to the bridegroom.

Jesus never simply told us to honor others more than ourselves; he lived it, and the cross was not the first time. Some person whom Jesus may or may not have known had a problem that wouldn't have haunted him all his days. His party may not have been remembered as the greatest, but that could blow over.

Yet Jesus saw it fit to provide this man with ample wine, and the best wine of the party at that. The gift arrived secretly and blessed abundantly and extravagantly. The giver asked nothing in return.

*Adam*

- Whom have you sought to bless recently, and what did you ask in return?

- In what circumstances do you look to bless people—only in the dire, or in the everyday and mundane situations? Why?

- Do you look for God's hand in your life and seek to give Him the credit He hasn't asked for?

**DAY 75**

# ENGLISH IS RELEVANT, AND SO IS JESUS

"As the centuries pass, the evidence is accumulating that, measured by his effect on history, Jesus is the most influential life ever lived on this planet."

—HISTORIAN KENNETH SCOTT LATOURETTE

| 1 Corinthians 3:10-15 | Philippians 3:7-16 | Hebrews 1:1-4, 2:1-4 |

"What does Shakespeare's Julius Caesar have to do with anything? Will I ever use this? Does this literature stuff matter at all?" My questions regularly flummoxed my high school English teachers. Convinced my classmates had the same questions, I voiced them regularly.

Five years and an English degree later, I stood before a group of high school freshmen teaching English literature. Life's irony is laughable. Convinced they'd have the same questions, I tried to head them off daily, answering before they could ask.

I sought to convey the relevance to their world. I invoked *Fight Club* and magazine ads. We discussed what they watched on TV or read in print. This stuff matters, and it touches all areas of life, I contended. Reading literature teaches us to read the world, to understand communication, ideas, symbols, beauty, and narrative.

Some eventually bought into it. At least their term-ending essays on what they learned that year said so.

It is the same with Jesus.

A barista I know sat down with me while I used his coffee shop for an office.

"You're into Jesus, huh?" he asked.

"Yeah. Yeah, I am."

"That's cool."

Because I'm convinced Jesus can be a lot of things but not merely cool, I asked, "What do you think about Him?"

"I like Jesus," he said, his voice trailing off, hoping to end the talk. I dropped it.

Cool? Cool as in far out, maybe. Cool as in just another chill dude? No. He doesn't allow room merely to be cool.

Have you read what He said? He said the poor are blessed. We hate poverty. We look the other way when the poor beg on our streets. We don't want to deal with them. Jesus said love your enemies. We hate our enemies. And if we can't destroy them, we at least want them to be agreeable. He said to take the place of least honor. We want all the honor for ourselves, because we know no one else will look out for us.

Jesus cannot be cool by our standards. Because everything he says matters if it's true. It touches and demands access to all areas of our lives: time, money, career, sexuality, relationships, thoughts, motives, words, hopes, and heart.

As literature teaches us to look for meaning, to seek out answers, it offers us indispensable tools for life. It is relevant. Jesus teaches us all the above, and He confronts every critical issue we face. Now that's relevant.

*Amy*

---

- To what extent does Jesus matter in your life?
- How do His words affect you if they're true?
- What is Jesus' most challenging exhortation? Is it relevant to you?

# DAY 76

# WANTING FOR MORE

"There is no good applying to Heaven for earthly comfort. Heaven can give heavenly comfort, no other kind."

—C. S. LEWIS

| 2 Corinthians 5:1-4 | Matthew 13:44 | Philippians 3:14-15 |

Have you ever wanted heaven because you grew sick of sin in this world? It may have simply inhabited the air around you, or you may have tripped over it too many times. Either way, it gave you a semi-nauseating feeling in your stomach.

You see it around you, in advertising, in movies and on television, and at almost any social event. You think, "There's got to be more than this. This is just disgusting and heartbreaking." You start to hate this non-life offered as a poor substitute for real life in this convoluted world.

Maybe we wrestle with a certain sin (or twenty) and inside we feel sad, broken, sick, frustrated, and angry because we did it, and we hoped and promised we would not, and yet we did. And maybe we start to loathe part of ourselves.

Some spiritual guru who wrote a best-selling how-to book yelled out, "Try harder! Just believe! You will overcome all sin in this world if you just believe, obey, and pray more! And buy my book!" Some of the most spiritual people I know, many with their hand on death's doorknob, still struggle with sin. It remains a thorn in their side. And it's painful, so painful that the only thing any of us wants is to be rid of it.

I don't know if anyone overcomes sin completely, but even if they do, its presence in the world still remains, still darkens the days. It exists. We all want something more than this fractured way of being. We can have confidence, however, that this sickness will not last forever. We were not made for this world. This sickness we feel tells us as much as what the Scriptures confirm: things are not right here. This is not our home. In the 1980s movie *E.T.* the extra-terrestrial being constantly asked to phone home. He implied he wasn't from here. Home was somewhere else, and part of the redemptive process we experience regarding sin is an increase in our longing for our real home.

This can happen because God remains larger than the sadness, evil, and pain in our world. And He takes the bad, and in it He tells us He's still in charge, and He pulls good from it. That good is this longing.

Pain will come. Sin will cripple. It will hang like a foul odor. But we are going to leave all sin behind one day, and because of that, we can hold onto hope. We can continue, confident that the status quo will not remain. Thus, we strive against sin. This very striving battles against sin in the self, and this striving battles against sin in the world. The earth will never be heaven. Yet we can find in our sadness and disgust with sin a longing that makes for something good and true and right. That's redemption. And that wanting for heaven might bring a little of heaven to us.

*Amy*

---

- How does sin make you feel?
- To what extent do you respond to it with a desire for something more?
- What does your longing for something better produce in your life?

# DAY 77

# IMAGO DEI

"So tell me what I see when I look in your eyes; is that you baby, or just a brilliant disguise?"

—BRUCE SPRINGSTEEN

| Genesis 1:26-27 | Luke 15:11-32 | 1 John 3:2 |

In His own image He created them (see Genesis 1:27). In the image of God He made them. In His image He made you and me.

A not exactly attractive girl stood at the counter waiting for the clerk to make change for her. She looked over her shoulder to the row of tables and their guests facing her. Her eyes met those of a young man at one of the tables. She smiled. Would he smile back at her? Physical beauty is esteemed. We offer little attention to what is not attractive. Her smile, though, revealed to him the truth, a truth not dependent on his reaction of approval or disdain. She was made by God. God had her in mind. And God smiled when He looked upon her. Despite her lack of physical beauty, beauty made her and resided there. He had cast her in His own image. He recognized the picture of God she carried; he smiled with gratitude, with admiration. For she reflected God's image.

The dying man lay on a bed in Calcutta. He'd been there a week and had maybe one more left in him. His impoverished life was evident by his weathered body. Wasted, worn, wracked with pain, this body had lived hard and alone. And now his nails needed clipping. The young nun cupped his heel softly, looked at him gently, and smiled. One by one, she clipped his toenails. She saw the image of God.

The uniqueness of God's creation and creativity resides within each of us. Like snowflakes, each person has an individual stamp, a mark of singularity, and personal attention from the Creator. Thus, each person merits our attention and respect. Yet to see the image of God in each other, we must look beyond skin color, socioeconomic status, clothing, age, weight, and even behavior and attitudes in order to see the handiwork of God. It takes time and discipline to learn to see others like this. It takes patience to look until you actually see.

We bear His image. Will we recognize this in each other? Will we help one another believe in our identity as image-bearers of God? When we see the homeless man begging at the intersection or the lobbyist walking the statehouse halls, do we see the image of God? The young couple trying to pay its mortgage, the pastor struggling with his children, the single mother putting herself through school, the president of the United States all bear the image of God. We need to see that.

Others need that from us. We need that from each other. May we begin looking that we might see each other as God sees us, and in so doing, see more of His love in this world.

*Amy*

---

- **What are the implications of believing someone bears God's image?**
- **How does this change how we see them, interact with them?**
- **How does this change us?**

# DAY 78

# STANDARDS

"I have never read any theologian who claims
that God is particularly interested in religion anyways."

—ANNIE DILLARD

| Luke 9:51-56 | Luke 13:22-30 | John 21:20-22 |

Killing time in an airport, I struck up a conversation with a stranger. When asked what I do, I told this man that I write about Jesus' teachings. The man, hearing the name Jesus fired off questions: "Do you believe Jesus is the Son of God? That He shed His blood for our sins? That He died and rose again? That we will be with Him forever if we repent and are baptized?" I forgot a few in the litany because his machine-gun delivery leveled me.

This guy wanted to see if I passed the test. Was I in or out? Were we friends or enemies? One of "them" or one of "us"? Did I believe correctly? Did I believe the right things?

My test-wielding friend mirrors the rigor of an Ivy League admissions committee. Would I uphold all sorts of standards? My humble applications never made it to any of those committees at Yale, Brown, or Harvard. The intern in the admissions office cashed my application check, glanced at my SAT score, chuckled, and then sent my ten-page application and essays to the recycle bin.

But Jesus didn't do any of this. When He selected followers, He chose the rejects. His membership requirements defied human logic. He let everyone in, never pre-qualifying the crowds he taught. They had not confessed that He was the Messiah. They had neither matriculated through a proper course of study, nor walked the Romans Road. In fact, they had not yet read any of the New Testament. How could these people properly handle His teaching without the prerequisites?

Yet anyone who came with a question, He taught. Whenever and with whomever He was at dinner He taught. He seemed to think what He taught was the point, and that everyone needed to hear it, regardless of their background, religion (Samaritans?! Are you kidding?!), social standing (sinful women?!), or righteousness knowledge of the texts. Not all stayed, but all were given opportunity to hear what He said. He just taught. And He let the teachings set the standards. His teachings came across hard and direct. The people would sort themselves out according to their desire to follow, according to their recognition of their own needs. It's still that way.

Jesus didn't seek to exclude. He sought to include everyone in the kingdom who desired it. Nothing they had or had not done could disqualify someone seeking, sometimes even someone barely seeking. Jesus wanted them to come to Him. He still does.

The teachings are the point. Our qualifications are not.

*Amy*

---

- **Do you try to figure out if people are "in" or "out"? What does it look like?**
- **Is that what we're supposed to do?**
- **To what extent have we been taught wrongly about judging people's beliefs?**

# DAY 79

# INCOMPLETE PEOPLE

> When I get honest, I admit I am a bundle of paradoxes. I believe and I doubt, I hope and get discouraged, I love, and I hate, I feel bad about feeling good, I feel guilty about not feeling guilty. I am trusting and suspicious. I am honest and I still play games. Aristotle said I am a rational animal; I say I am an angel with an incredible capacity for beer."
>
> —BRENNAN MANNING

| Philippians 3:7-14 | Hebrews 12:1-2 | Colossians 3:1-4 |

One man loves well, but he cannot manage money. She manages money but struggles to care for her husband. He cares for his family and serves in his community but is addicted to work. She loves the Lord but drinks herself to sleep at night. She swears and smokes and has a short temper but has a soft and generous heart. He's defensive and fearful but passionate about justice and mercy. He gives to the poor, cares for orphans and widows, but struggles with pornography.

This is who we are. We are a people in process. We are all incomplete.

Yet why then do we fight to disbelieve that we should be complete? Why do we hate ourselves for unachieved completion? Have we ever looked critically at the people whom God loved, chose, honored, and befriended?

Elijah complained about the situations he endured as God's prophet. Noah, God's choice for saving humanity during the flood, on at least one occasion drank himself unconscious. Jacob, the father of Israel, lied and cheated. Moses killed a man, fled justice, and failed to believe God's promise about bringing water from a rock. But he also led God's people out of slavery in Egypt. Jonah, whom God used to speak to a city of 500,000, attempted to escape because he was afraid and ran from God. David took another man's wife, and when she became pregnant, killed her husband, one of his most loyal soldiers. Yet the Bible still regards David as a "man after God's own heart" (1 Samuel 13:14). Solomon, full of wisdom, followed his wives to other gods. God chose him to build His temple. Samson, on whom the Spirit of God rested, wrought destruction everywhere he went. Abraham, always terrified and lying to save himself, heard God's call to be father of the nations. Peter betrayed Jesus three times. Jesus named him the Rock. Paul persecuted the early followers of Jesus, overseeing their executions. He then wrote the majority of the New Testament.

Some lived badly and transformed into good. Some lived well and behaved badly at times. The Lord has a history of claims on both types of people. But these people God loved. These people God continued to shape, to embrace, to teach. We know these people because we are these people. We cheat, steal, lie, fornicate, gamble, lust, kill, betray, persecute, complain, run, seek false gods, destroy, hate. The list goes on. But so does His love and His careful attention to our growth and maturation.

We're incomplete. But only for now. The God who chose us has not done so simply because He needed work done in the world. He chose us because He wants work done in us. And He's still busy doing it, preparing us to live as we engage in the process.

*Amy*

---

- To whom do you decline love and mercy because their process frustrates you?
- How can you offer yourself forgiveness in this? How can you offer the same to others in process?

**DAY 80**

# FOR THE WORLD?

"As I observe the tribal differences, religious divisions, poverty and disease, lack of sufficient educational opportunities for our children, political upheaval and strife, it becomes obvious that the principles of Jesus Christ have not penetrated Africa enough!"

—UGANDAN PRESIDENT YOWERI MUSEVENI, SPEAKING TO OTHER AFRICAN LEADERS

| Matthew 17:20 | Luke 12:22-34 | Luke 7:21-23 |

Is He enough for this world? Can He heal divisions in my church? In my country? In my government? On my team? In my office? In my household? Between India and Pakistan? Between Muslims and Christians? Between Democrat and Republican? Between black churches and white churches? Between Palestinians and Israelis? Between oil barons and greenies?

Is there really neither Greek nor Jew in Him? Rich nor poor? Catholic nor Protestant? Capitalist nor communist?

Jock nor geek? Haves nor have-nots? Shiite nor Sunni? Is He enough?

Is Jesus enough today? Is Jesus enough to both rise from the dead and overturn man's laws? Or do we need to rely on lobbyists and the Supreme Court for that? Is Jesus enough to create the world and end human trafficking? Or should we pin our hopes on the UN and NGOs?

Can the Jesus who fed five thousand with two fish and five loaves still feed the hungry? Can Jesus, who healed the blind and cured the lepers, defeat AIDS?

Can He who calmed the waters heal the planet's wounds, or should we hold out for Kyoto? Can the one who said He'd bring all men to Himself reconcile Turks and Armenians, Russians and Ukrainians, North and South Korea? Can He heal South Africa? Can the one who gave the Spirit also guide America wisely?

Can He who tells us that the kingdom is near teach us not to build our own empires? Can the one whose love drives out fear bring peace in the midst of terrorism? Can He who cast out demons cast them out now?

Can He who raised the temple in three days bring down the sex industries of Vegas and Thailand? Can He who tells us to love also redeem the hearts of those engaging in torture? What of tsunamis? Floods? Kidnappings? Beheadings? Rape? Corporate corruption? Tribal warfare at home and abroad? Widow burning? Is He enough?

Do we barely stammer a yes for fear of not having enough faith? Do we qualify our yes with "As long as peace talks work, NATO involves itself, the right people are in office, the market picks up, we cut emissions, bills are passed, hearts change miraculously"? Would these answers we offer ever be enough?

Or do we believe so much in certain views of Scriptures that we've never dared dream He could or would do such if asked? If believed? Do we believe in Him? Is He enough?

*Adam*

## DAY 81

# IS HE ENOUGH FOR ME?

> "'I Am the Way' is based on music that resolves, because Jesus is the resolver. Jesus is the solution to all our problems. People haven't changed in 2,000 years. They have the same problems today as the Bible characters did."
>
> —JEROME HINES,
> WRITER OF "I AM THE WAY"

| 2 Corinthians 12:7-10 | John 3:16-21 (esp. 17) | Ephesians 3:14-21 |

Is Jesus enough for me? Is He enough to bring me back? Or do I need the right church, the right books, the right job, or the right pastor? Do I need the proper friends? Do I need to dress a certain way and attend certain conventions while eschewing certain words?

He led a people out of Egypt. Can He lead me out of the slavery of my wounds and past? Do I need counselors, exercise, and medications for this? Can Jesus make me patient, kind, good, loving, joyful, peaceful, gentle, faithful, and self-controlled? Or will that merely happen "with time"?

Can this friend of sinners help me through divorce? Sexual abuse? Alcoholism? Adultery? Addiction? A broken self-image? Bankruptcy? Failed businesses and a shattered career? Self-righteousness? Arrogance? Pride? A desire to steal? A habit of deceit? Can He who rose from the dead also resurrect me from rejection? Should I look to meditation and retreats for these?

Can He who forgave Peter help me love friends who betrayed me? Can this friend of outcasts help me see beauty in those who are different or just a little off? Is He enough to overcome the ego that rules me? Is He enough to overcome my need for affirmation or my compulsion to follow anyone who offers attention? Can He deal with my fears? Can He lead me out of the past? Can He help me forgive myself? Or am I on my own?

Can He who sent the adulterous woman away new also make me new?

What's more, can He love me, who is broken, abused, addicted? Me, who steals, lies, curses, wounds, and lusts? Me, who stumbles, falls, fails, and then judges others for the same?

Is He enough to uncover something magnificent inside me? Is He enough to help me believe that I possess goodness and beauty? Or will I continue to dislike who I am and believe myself ugly? Can He teach me that He sees me otherwise? Can He help me see myself otherwise? Can He who asked Peter, "Where is your faith?" give me faith?

Is He bigger than my doctrine? My religion? My possessions? My view of the world? My needs and hurts? My prejudices? Is He big enough?

To what extent is Jesus enough for *me*?

*Adam*

# DAY 82

# WHO I AM

"But you are who you are."

—STEPHEN KELLOGG AND THE SIXERS,
"CRADLE OF FAMILY"

| Matthew 10 | Romans 8:12-17 | Isaiah 43:1-7 |

Throughout Dixie, I'm a Tennessean. Folks in Georgia and Alabama know what that means. Outside the South, I'm a Southerner. That means something to Yankees. Around the world, I'm American. That means something to everyone I meet off native soil.

Wars, stalled climate accords, and rumors of torture made me wary of what people in other countries thought of America or Americans. Despite my concerns I still traveled with some friends to Norway to see a friend.

Expecting to face bitterness, I found people who genuinely liked Americans. Anticipating indifference and even hostility, I discovered people shy about, but fond of, American gregariousness. Thinking they would detest everything American,

I heard our music in every club and restaurant. I glimpsed our movies advertised everywhere. And I saw our businesses on all corners.

I felt like a member of a club. So much of what the people loved came from my country; and that made me proud. I bear a family resemblance to this cultural juggernaut. I'm American. That word, that identity, feels like power in conversation: it changes every dynamic. Because of this, I possessed a little swagger in my personal interactions.

But the American identity doesn't revolve solely around the word *America*. I carried the identity within me. It gave me confidence.

I believe that Jesus' name immediately re-draws the contours of any conversation. Bringing Him up alters the course of discussion at once, just as being American does. If mentioning Him results in a positive response, so much the better. If not, my surly nature prepares for a fight.

I am proud of Jesus, but do I say His name with boldness as I do for America? His name feels like power on my tongue, but do I hesitate to speak it?

His name will not come up in every conversation. I say my primary association is with Him. Does that instill me with such confidence as I meet people, engage them, wander the world? Am I aware of what it means to be a follower of Jesus? Does that mean something, and if so, what?

Perhaps it means something to others. Perhaps it means something different to everyone I meet. But what does it mean to me?

*Adam*

- How does your association with Jesus alter your view of yourself?
- How do you feel toward your ethnic or national identity?
- What does your country's name mean to others? What does Jesus' name mean to them?

# DAY 83

# LEARNING

"The question of whether or not we arrive at a particular goal is of little importance, and reaching it becomes merely an episode along the way. What we see as only the process of reaching a particular end, God sees as the goal itself."

—OSWALD CHAMBERS

| Matthew 7:7-11 | Philippians 4:8-9 | 1 Corinthians 3:1-4 |

Why do so many colleges exist? Does our nation truly contain such an extensive number of eager learners who wish to dedicate four years of their lives to study?

Complaints over reading assignments and groaning over required papers cause me to think otherwise. I observe the parties and intense social hierarchies that abound throughout campus, making it appear more like a prolonged, inebriated vacation under the guise of academic pursuit.

We do not want to engage our minds. We want the easy answers that someone else developed. We want to memorize and regurgitate. We want the multiple-choice test, not the ambiguous essay response. And we can have this. We can graduate high school and college without ever really learning. We can survive. But perhaps there is more. Perhaps we can struggle and question and endeavor. Perhaps we can think.

Yet thinking is hard, and learning is terrifying in the most beautiful way.

We may learn the uncontainable bigness of the world. Its potential dangers and infinite possibilities of beauty most certainly threaten to exceed our confined expectations. In ancient times, young Jewish boys went to the synagogues and began to study the Torah (the first five books of the Old Testament) at six years old. By the end of their education, they had memorized it in its entirety. These adolescent competitors begged their teachers (rabbis) to allow them the privilege of reading the texts aloud. They associated learning with something sacred and beautiful. It was desirable and sweet, like the honey the teachers placed on their fingers to remind them of the allure of God.

In these schools of learning, the children strived to not only know the answers to the questions, but to know intimately the questions themselves. The rabbi would ask, "What is two plus two?"

In response the student would ask, "What is sixteen divided by four?" or "What is three plus one?" To answer with these advanced responses, one must launch the brain into logical progressions.

Jesus taught in the same way. He answered a question with a question. Frustration ensued for His followers. If He had provided just an answer, something would have escaped in the process: the lessons of the process itself.

We are supposed to grapple, struggle, and discern. Perhaps the questions baffle us because they have no answer. Perhaps the answer is multiple questions away from the original. The learning lies in the journey. Will you learn?

*Amy*

---

- **Why do we resist learning?**
- **How can we develop a desire to grow?**
- **How do we learn the best lessons?**

# DAY 84

# KNOWING, LOVING, LOOKING

"Faith is the gaze of the soul upon a saving God."

—A. W. TOZER

| John 14:7-17 | Hebrews 12:2 | 2 Timothy 1:12 |

Sometimes when I drive across the Naval Academy Bridge, I must steer my eyes toward the brake lights in front of me. The glistening water to my right and the drifting sailboats headed east in slow freedom plead for my attention. An almost magnetic force freezes the gazes of a bride and groom as they look adoringly into one another's eyes. While engrossed in a gripping novel, looking away from the pages of my vice and engaging with whomever just walked into the room is like prying myself out of bed at an unhealthy hour.

It seems that the ability to focus on something with our eyes is one of the easiest things in the world to do, with one important stipulation—we must be wildly interested in the object of our attention. When our interest in something is less than passionate, our attention to that object wanders.

In his essay, "The Gaze of the Soul," A. W. Tozer describes faith as "the gaze of the soul upon a saving God." Drawing upon biblical references to looking and believing, he contends that these two actions are identical in the spiritual life.

Paul offers a similar understanding of faith. His exhortation to look "only at Jesus," (Hebrews 12:2) comes immediately after a long and thorough demonstration of the faith of early believers. Readers of Hebrews 11 might throw up their hands in despair and question how and if they could ever exercise such bold faith. Paul's response is simple: in order to believe, look at Jesus with the eyes of your heart. To look closely, adoringly, and continuously at Jesus, our affection for Him must increase.

Often our attempts to increase our faith remain nothing more than vague efforts to believe more, trust more. While these are honorable goals, they often leave us wondering, "But how?" What if the means to increasing our faith were actually fixing our attention on the astounding compassion of God or His unfathomable wisdom? What if we sought to really and truly know the character of the most fascinating and worthy one? Falling in love with Him more will certainly require persistence, for His great depths aren't always as instantly gratifying or apparent as a 6 a.m. sky painted yellow, orange, and purple. But what if our love for Him increased so much that when someone broke our heart, or we totaled our car or lost our job, we just couldn't steal our attention away from Him long enough to doubt His control and concern?

We can't gaze at God intently without loving Him first. And we can't love Him without knowing Him. Faith begins with knowledge and then follows with love that can't take its eyes off the beloved.

And this is the faith that will boldly declare, "I know whom I have believed, and I am convinced that he is able to guard what I have entrusted to Him until that day" (2 Timothy 1:12).

*Liz*

---

- How do you know others?
- What increases your affection for them?
- How might this pertain to your relationship with Jesus, as well?

# DAY 85

# SOMETHING BROKEN

> "Week after week Christ washes the disciples' dirty feet, handles their very toes, and repeats. It is all right—believe it or not—to be people. Who can believe it?"
>
> —ANNIE DILLARD

| John 12:23-26 | Colossians 2:20-23 | Romans 12:1-8 (esp. 2) |

Our natural inclination expects perfection. We crave it, not because we've ever known something perfect, but because we think we should. My car breaks down and frustration ensues. My sister hurts me or fails to follow through on a promise. I'm disillusioned and jaded. Plans fall apart, and dreams sometimes vanish in the face of reality. I stand discontent and constantly berate myself. I'm not good enough, smart enough, pretty enough, confident enough, witty enough, worthy enough.

I'm not perfect. They are not perfect. It is not perfect.

We are not home.

And perhaps that simple statement, that obvious, yet elusive truth, brings freedom. If we are not home, if this is not heaven, then perfection is not our natural state. This world exists in brokenness. Those glimmering times of wholeness merely serve as reminders that there is something more.

Years ago I sat in church as ushers handed out roses to the congregation. The pastor explained that these flowers should serve as a reminder to pray for someone or something specific. When God answered the prayer, we were to return the flower so it could be included in a wreath.

Questions arose from the members. "How?" "Why?" Then someone asked a pertinent question. "What if we prayed for someone sick and they died?"

The pastor paused thoughtfully and offered a response. "Is that not the ultimate healing?" He posed to the congregation. "Are we not only temporarily well?"

These words return to me when I battle the flu. They provide insight when I limp around with a stress fracture. I tangibly experience and view my humanity. I am temporarily well just as this world is temporarily well.

We are not home yet.

I ponder this thought and demand more from it than a simple salve for a disillusioned existence. Paradoxically, I want more because I want less. I want more life through my acknowledgement of less perfection.

When I release my world from the standard of perfection, I live in freedom. No longer do people need to perform flawlessly and serve our friendships with infallible faithfulness. I can allow them their humanity, not in apathetic concession to imperfection, but in the mutual understanding of our shared failings.

*Amy*

- From what do you demand perfection in your life?
- How does this standard affect your relationships? Your perspective? Your heart?
- What does it mean to want more?

# DAY 86

# THE ROAD HOME

*"If I find myself a desire
that nothing in this world can satisfy
it must mean that I was made for another world."*

—C.S. LEWIS

| 2 Corinthians 5 | John 14:1-14 | Luke 15:11-32 |

Returning from vacation, I drive down the same roads, knowing each sharp turn and pothole. I know just when to press the gas and the perfect braking pattern to round the last turn. I pull into the garage and unload. Opening the door to the house, it creaks in the same way. A familiar smell arouses my senses.

At nighttime, I walk the darkened hallways, knowing the number of stairs to the top and the location of the end table. (I bumped into it too many times.) I don't need the light.

I am home.

Beyond these tangibles, home carries the familiarity of people and identity: the sound of Dad grinding coffee beans in the early morning, unmandated gatherings in the living room, memories. At home we rest not only our bodies but also our souls. We find solace in the familiar, unchanging nature.

What is home? A place? People? Friends? Family? Identity? Yes. But it is also something more, something that eludes description.

Wikipedia offers the paltry definition of a dwelling place and then provides the picture of a house. A house fails to fully describe a home. Wikipedia knows this and as a result attempts to supplement the incomplete with popular sayings about the concept: "Home is where the heart is." "There's no place like home." "Home sweet home."

We return to the initial question: What is home? And why do we so desperately want to go there? How?

In the *Odyssey*, Homer weaves the tale of Odysseus, a brave soldier returning to his homeland, Ithaca, after the ten-year Trojan War. On his journey he encounters enemies, mortal and immortal, who attempt to prevent his homecoming. Calypso, a seductive goddess, traps Odysseus on her island indefinitely with the provision of endless passion and paradise. Yet each day Odysseus, the weathered fighter, cries wrenching tears. Even in bliss he just wants to go home. Palm trees and lusty nights fail to fulfill that unfulfilled longing.

Calypso questions him. Is his wife superior to her in stature or beauty?

"No." He assures her. "You, Calypso, are superior in every way."

She questions his reasonings again. All Odysseus can provide is that he wants to go home because he wants to go home.

Is it possible to miss somewhere I have never been? I want to go home. I miss home. And I know that this world is not it. Does my longing indicate an existence even if I cannot fully explain? Must I forget in order to remember? Must I look past the tangible elements that attempt to distract in order to see the intangible promise of home?

*Amy*

---

- What is home? Where is it?
- Why do you want to go there?
- What distractions prevent you from wanting home?

# DAY 87

# WHEN I THINK OF HEAVEN

"I think of you, do you think of me?"

—COUNTING CROWS,
"RAIN KING"

| Revelation 21, 22 | Daniel 7:11-14 | Daniel 7:26-27 | Matthew 5:1-20 |

In heaven, I think…
 Celebrities won't be as weird as they are here, and politicians won't be as insecure.
 NBA players will play hard all eighty-two games.
 Beer will be cheap at concerts, pro sports games, and fall festivals.
 The Ryder Cup will be evenly matched every year.
 Healthy food will taste great.
 NCAA football will work properly, resulting in an eight-team playoff.
 All barbeque will come from Memphis.
 We'll never cork the wine.
 All customers at restaurants will tip servers well.

That's some of what I think.

This is what I really think, though. In heaven, we'll be able to watch the sunrise. Heavy eyes won't need to shut.

We won't worry about making more money for a rainy day. The rainy days that do come will be for mud games and stomping in puddles.

We won't struggle with the pressure of holding an acceptable job.

Flies will stay away from our food, and our cups of tea and coffee.

We will run because we enjoy it, not to carve an acceptable body. When we do run, joints won't hurt, ankles won't turn, and bones won't ache.

We'll need not say, "I wish I had more time." We'll have plenty.

Cosmetic surgery won't exist. We'll be happy with how we look.

We won't "have to run" to a meeting or appointment. We'll be able to stay.

Fear won't dictate our days.

Our misdirected appetites won't drive us. Love will.

In heaven, depression won't visit us. And we won't need medications.

I think we'll be able to listen to each other and to God without distractions.

*Adam*

- Do you think about heaven?
- What do you think?
- How does this change how we think about life in this world?

# DAY 88

# FORGET TO REMEMBER

"Maybe the God who offered everything,
at the same time demanded everything."

—FREDERICK BUECHNER

| Deuteronomy 8:1-18 | John 6 | Psalm 78 |

As a kid, I loved the book, *Cloudy with a Chance of Meatballs*. I loved its vertically rectangular cover that opened to reveal an enticing world of possibility. I loved the sketch drawings that evoked vivid wonder.

The land of Chewandswallow existed many oceans and expansive deserts away. In that utopia, the townspeople never visited the grocery store. Restaurants had no menus nor roofs and supplied only plates and utensils to their patrons. In that town, the food fell from the sky three times a day. Breakfast. Lunch. Dinner. Meteorologists forecasted meals instead of precipitation. "Cloudy with a chance of meatballs." "Sunny with a pea soup fog in the morning and hamburger clouds descending in the afternoon."

My mind reeled with the suggestion of such a place. I turned each page with excitement, curious and intrigued by what type of culinary precipitation was yet to come. Until one day when the weather went awry. Overcooked broccoli rained down for days. An inundation of syrup flooded the city streets. A giant pancake buried the library. Officials canceled school. With childhood terror I turned page after page of Chewandswallow destruction. Chewandswallow was lost in excess.

I am similarly lost in excess. I am lost in the façade of preparation and control. Food lines the refrigerator. I am ready, dependent on whims and whimsies of nothing and no one.

As I grew up and the mystique of Chewandswallow faded, I determined that those people lived a confined existence. They lacked control, unable to choose their daily meal. But what does this supposed control give me? Freedom? Or just its appearance?

Perhaps they lived in freedom, freedom to trust and freedom from the details and minutiae of sustenance. Perhaps I, too, have this choice, not to wait expectantly with my cereal bowl and spoon in the front yard at sunrise, for a shower of Cheerios and a sprinkling of milk, but to choose freedom of faith instead of control.

Food fell from the sky years ago. The Israelites wandered in the desert, exiles walking toward an unseen promised land. And God sustained them. In desolate wilderness, He rained down manna every morning and every night. It arrived consistently, and the people still feared. They feared it would not come.

Then they chose control. They hoarded the manna, stashing it away in tent corners. The manna rotted. Maggots teemed on the once heavenly provision. God gives us enough for today. Tomorrow more will arrive. So why do I doubt?

*Amy*

---◆---

- ☐ **To what extent do you believe in daily provision?**
- ☐ **Do you choose freedom or control? How? Why?**
- ☐ **Why is it hard to trust?**

## DAY 89

# LIFE THROUGH CREATION

"The more you're like yourself the less you're like others. You're not alive unless you're creating."

—WALT DISNEY

| Genesis 1 | Genesis 5:1-3 | Ephesians 2:1-10 (esp. 10) |

The Bible begins with creation. God creates something from nothing and transforms void into vastness. Light differentiates from darkness. Land separates from the sea. Trees, plants, and animals are given life and placed in the newness newly created.

Then God crafts His most artistic work: man. He sculpts the form and imbues a specific gift and unique purpose: creativity and the ability to create. He allows man to give birth, both to offspring and to ideas. While man cannot imitate God in the creation of something from nothing, He can create something from something.

He thus becomes artist and cocreator with God.

It's scary to admit that you're an artist: to reveal yourself as a singer, a writer, a poet, a musician. People will want you to draw, sing, write, compose, or perform for them. We prefer to slink into predefined roles of rote routine and definable ends. We prefer to hide and resist our calling to create, afraid we might have nothing to show or that others will disapprove of our art and consequently disapprove of us.

Creating requires effort. Creating requires dedication. Creating requires unswerving focus through a long, demanding process.

Beethoven, although deaf, composed symphonies in an unlikely way. He cut the legs off his piano and felt the reverberations of each note on the ground. Annie Dillard wrote her Pulitzer Prize-winning novel locked in a cabin living off chocolate and Coke. Michelangelo painted the masterful ceiling of the Sistine Chapel by laying on his back for days, paint falling on his face, on a shaky scaffolding high aloft. These masters gave themselves to their purpose. They physically suffered for the creation of something beautiful, something unheard, unread, undiscovered, before they themselves produced it. Creating requires effort.

I know when I am creating. And I know when I am imitating. I know the difference between something original and something copied both in my writing and in myself.

God created me to create.

He created me with a desire to make something—something as definable as art or something as intangible as a friendship. He created me to know myself and to know Him through this outward manifestation of my internal self.

But this scares me.

Knowing God feels like unmapped terrain or uncharted waters. To know myself signifies the release of control over what I may discover. I may travel places, in my life and in my heart, where the end proves unseen. I may discover—no—I will most certainly discover that I am unique. Yet in this uniqueness I am just like everybody else in his or her own inexplicable uniqueness.

I am created to create. I am born to live. I am called to live a purpose out of my unique gifts and talents. Will I?

*Amy*

---

- What does it mean to create in your life?
- What fears hold you back?
- What are we supposed to create? How?

# DAY 90

# THE WEDDING AT CANA

"Random acts of kindness in fact
reflect the heart of God."

—ANONYMOUS

| John 2:1-11 | John 3:30 | Proverbs 11:24-25 |

Two things strike me when I read about the miracle of Jesus turning water into wine. The physical transformation stands out, for sure, but it's the nature of the circumstances sparking the miracle that catches my attention. The event says something specific about Jesus as a person.

I don't claim exhaustive expertise on the ancient Near East, or even on Jewish culture and customs. I have difficulty understanding why Jesus' mother thought He should involve Himself. Certainly any host would feel a little embarrassed to run out of provisions for all his guests, but does this really qualify as a moment for divine intervention? Doesn't the Lord have more important things on His agenda than an open bar?

Yet Mary thought this merited the attention of her son. So she said, "They have no wine." She didn't say anything else, but from Jesus' response, we can tell she implied more.

"They have a problem, and they need help. The bridegroom certainly does, given that some of his reputation rests on how well he can entertain. Won't you help them?"

Mary had a precious sensitivity. Jesus possessed one as well and saw fit to bless the people at the wedding in general, and the bridegroom in particular. The opportunity he chose, providing more wine, wasn't one of life or death. But it communicated affection.

Jesus provided somewhere between 120 and 180 gallons of the finest wine, depending on the size of the waterpots. Yet who received the credit for this wine? The bridegroom.

"The head waiter called the bridegroom, and said to him, 'Every man serves the good wine first, and when the people have drunk freely, then he serves the poorer wine; but you have kept the good wine until now.'"

Honor fell on this man. Jesus chose to receive no credit for the gift of the wine. He didn't ask for any sort of gratitude. He gave even that to the bridegroom.

Jesus never simply told us to honor others more than ourselves; he lived it, and the cross was not the first time. Some fellow whom Jesus may or may not have known had a problem that might have haunted him all his days.

Jesus saw it fit to provide this man with ample wine, and the best wine of the party, at that. The gift arrived secretly and blessed abundantly and extravagantly. The giver asked nothing in return.

*Adam*

- Whom have I sought to bless recently, and what did I ask in return?

- In what circumstances do I look to bless people: only in the most dire, or in the everyday and mundane?

- Do I look for God's hand in my life and seek to give Him the credit He hasn't asked for?

CPSIA information can be obtained
at www.ICGtesting.com
Printed in the USA
LVHW040657230123
737637LV00002B/4

9 781955 043847